"Passion changes the world. [...] people's creativity and product [...] puters. Wayne's passion is empowering people to make the impossible, possible. Read this book to find out how!"

Guy Kawasaki
Apple Fellow, author of How to Drive
Your Competition Crazy

"Wayne Allyn Root's message to Generation X: Practice discipline, teamwork, tenacity, and personal responsibility to succeed. It's an empowering message that he uses to motivate young people."

Haley Barbour
Chairman, Republican National Committee

"Wayne Root teaches what being an entrepreneur is all about—the ability to overcome failure and adversity. *The Joy of Failure!* gives you the tools to achieve the American Dream. This book is a must read!"

Charles Schwab
Chairman and CEO, The Charles Schwab Corporation

"There is a formula for success. Superachievers are not born; they are made. Wayne Root defines the principles that create superachievers."

Mac Anderson
CEO SUCCESSORIES

"As a former Super Bowl MVP and NFL Hall Of Famer, I can tell you with certaint that the best defense is a good offense. Wayne Root teaches anyone how to set big goals, design a winning game plan and then how to fight aggressively and passionately to make it happen. This program is like a playbook on how to achieve success at the game of life!"

Randy White
Member NFL Hall of Fame, member Dallas Cowboys Ring of Honor, Super Bowl MVP, Outland & Lombardi Trophy winner

"Leadership is all about vision, hope, energy, and inspiration. Wayne Root speaks the politics of success. He uplifts and empowers people all over the world."

Honorable Jerry Weller
U.S. congressman, Illinois

"The key to success in the television world is a creative and fertile imagination. That works in any field. You've got to think big to succeed. Wayne Allyn Root teaches businesspeople how to dream big and how to turn those dreams into reality."

Vin Di Bona
Television producer / creator, America's Funniest Home Videos, World's Funniest Videos

"If motivating a sales force is an art, Wayne Allyn Root is the Picasso of his day!"

Asher Dunn
CEO, Asher Dunn Estates Realty, Beverly Hills, CA, Prudential, Jon Douglas Real Estate Company

"As an entrepreneur and chief executive officer, I have found that the key to success is empowering employees to risk without fearing failure. No one teaches that lesson better than Wayne Root."

Carol Mercado
*CEO / entrepreneur, built three successful apparel companies
Recognized by* Redbook *magazine as Outstanding
Woman Entrepreneur*

"The job of an educator is to educate and enlighten—not only to provide knowledge, but also the inspiration and tools to apply that knowledge. Wayne Root's job is to empower people—to fill their hearts with inspiration, hope and the will to win. Wayne changes lives. He can change yours, too!"

Barry Stern, Ph.D.
*Director, Fast Track L.A., former deputy assistant secretary
for education under President Bush*

"Wayne Root's program brings together two unique forces in a very unique way. It combines a spiritual approach to helping individuals, along with a cognitive behavioral approach. To my knowledge this has never been done before."

Dr. Allen Berger, Ph.D.
Clinical director, Center for Counseling & Recovery

"Italians are known for their passion for life. Wayne Root teaches anyone how to live and work with passion."

Gianni Nunnari
President, Checchi Gori Pictures

"The real challenge facing most of us is creating inner beauty. When a person feels beautiful on the inside, their outer appearance follows suit. Wayne teaches a powerful course on how to create inner beauty. The result of this is the self-esteem to succeed at anything."

Karen Baldwin
Former Miss Universe, former Miss Canada

"Winners are easy to pick out in any field. In football you immediately think of Vince Lombardi, Tom Landry and Don Shula. In the field of corporate motivation, the name that comes to mind is Wayne Allyn Root. Wayne teaches executives how to give 110% and come out a winner every time."

Jack Snow
Voice of the St. Louis Rams, former NFL all-pro & Notre Dame all-American

"I've been around some of the greatest entertainers in Hollywood for several decades now. Wayne Root is a great performer too. But it isn't entertainment he's selling—it's empowerment!"

Bill Asher
Former award winning director, I Love Lucy, Gidget, Beach Blanket Bingo *and* Bewitched

"Wayne Root is like a great coach. He shows anyone how to be a champion. Wayne's program is a winner!"

Vlade Divac
NBA star, LA Lakers, Charlotte Hornets

"Wayne Root teaches us that with the gift of life comes the unlimited potential for greatness. Very few of us are able to reach our maximum potential. We need motivation and inspiration. Wayne's gift is that he motivates and inspires the greatness out of all of us."

Dr. Jon Franks, D.C.
World's only wheelchair triathlete, former NBA sports medicine consultant, former olympic boxing team chiropractor

"Coaches are critical to success. When we won the national championship, my coach was Barry Switzer. Now he's coach of the NFL Super Bowl Champion Dallas Cowboys. If your goal is winning at life, I'd recommend Wayne Allyn Root—He's a world class success coach."

Brian Bosworth
Action movie star, two time Butkus Award winner, Member, NCAA national championship team

"I've built one of the world's biggest telecommunications companies, employing thousands of people and I've lived my life using the principles that this program is based on—sound mind, sound body, positive attitude."

Jim Feist
CEO, Audio Communications, Inc.

"Wayne Root proves failure is merely a springboard to success."

Rieva Lesonsky
Editor-in-Chief, Entrepreneur *magazine*

"Life is like a football game. When you get knocked down, you have to get back up. And you must keep getting up until you score. The one who succeeds in this is the winner. Wayne Root teaches individuals how to get back up and score again and again!"

Anthony Davis

Two time college football all-American, member four NCAA championship teams, 1974 Heisman Trophy award runner-up

"The quality of one's life is determined by how well he or she deals with adversity. Adversity and challenge are experienced by the very rich, the very poor and everyone in between. Wayne Root teaches anyone the skills necessary to overcome challenges and excel at life."

John Lucas

Former NBA star, Former head coach San Antonio Spurs and Philadelphia 76ers

The Joy of Failure!

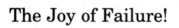

How to Turn Failure, Rejection, and Pain into Extraordinary Success

The Joy of Failure!

WAYNE ALLYN ROOT

THE SUMMIT PUBLISHING GROUP • ARLINGTON, TEXAS

THE SUMMIT PUBLISHING GROUP
One Arlington Centre
1112 East Copeland Road, Fifth Floor
Arlington, Texas 76011

Copyright © 1996 by Wayne Allyn Root

All rights reserved. No part of this book may be reproduced or transmitted in any form or by any means, electronic or mechanical, including photo-copying, recording, or by any information storage and retrieval system, without the written permission of the publisher, except where permitted by law.

Printed in the United States of America.

00 99 98 97 96   010   5 4 3 2 1

Library of Congress Cataloging-in-Publication Data
Root, Wayne Allyn.
    The joy of failure! : how to turn failure, rejection, and pain into
    extrordinary success / by Wayne Allyn Root.
        p. c.m.
    ISBN 1-56530-206-0
        1. Success. 2. Failure (Psychology) I. Title.
Bj1611.2.R587 1996
170'.44--dc21   96-45824
                                                            CIP

Cover and book design by David Sims
Cover photo by Lex Remlin

The Joy of Failure!
is dedicated to:

My father
DAVID ROOT
who taught me never to fear failure.

My mother
STELLA ROOT
who taught me the definition of tenacity.

My grandmother
META REIS
who taught me the meaning of courage and chutzpah.

My grandfather
SIMON REIS
who taught me the value of discipline.

My wife
DEBRA
and daughter
DAKOTA
who taught me the meaning of love.

*And most importantly to God—who inspired my words
and ideas and to whom I dedicate my life!*

Contents

Acknowledgments

First and foremost, my life is dedicated to God. Everything I do is for God, because of God, and dedicated to God. I thank God every day for the blessings He has bestowed upon me!

My next wave of thanks must go to my family—without their love and support, I'd be lost. Thank you to my wife Debra, the light of my life. Thank you for being there when I needed you, through all the stress and strain, the late nights of writing, rewriting, and rewriting again. I may be a professional motivator, but you are my motivation! Then of course, there's my daughter, Dakota Skye Root—the most beautiful and perfect child on earth. I swear I'm not biased—if you knew her, you'd think the same thing! She is the reason I work so hard—to ensure her future happiness and prosperity. Special thanks to my dogs, Bo and Kita, for always being there, with no demands and no agenda. Thanks to Ralph and Martha, my father- and mother-in-law, who after the death of my parents made me feel like I had a mom and dad again! Thanks to my sister Lori and my brother-in-law Doug—we've been through a lot together and I will always love you and be there for you. Thanks to my siblings-in-law Darla and Charlie (good luck on your mission—God bless you). And then there's the family no longer with me on earth—to my mother and father, David and Stella Root, and my grandparents, Meta and Simon Reis, thank you for watching over me as I put your words of wisdom to paper. I felt your presence. I miss you and I feel your love on a daily basis. I will love you always.

Thanks to all of the staff at The Summit Publishing Group who made this book possible. Special thanks to Len Oszustowicz, publisher; Mark Murphy, editor; and Bill Scott, associate editor, who saw the potential and then made it all happen. You are truly my definition of THRIVERS!

Thanks to all the friends and business associates who have nurtured and empowered me every step of the way in this long journey. A special word of thanks to my attorney, Lee Sacks—a rare combination of warrior and spiritual guide; my friend and infomercial producer John Berzner—who has guided me toward so many positive connections, without expecting anything in return; and all the support staff at ROOT INTERNATIONAL—you are loved and appreciated. No acknowledgment could be complete without a special note of thanks to two very special people: Doug Miller, my dearest friend and mentor, for all your advice and counsel over the years, and for your faith in my talents—even when all others jumped ship, you were always there! And to Jim Feist, my friend and business partner. Your words of wisdom have greatly enriched my life. Thank you for believing in my talents and giving me a starring role on your television show. Because of you, the last six years have been the best years of my life!

A few others there at the very beginnings of *The Joy of Failure!* and to whom I owe a debt of gratitude— Matthew Schiff (I've failed my way to the top; you're next!), Peter Paul, Jesse Rosenfeld, Petar Lasic, my agent Jim Hess, Lou Caruso, and my good friend Asher Dann. (Richard and Starr, now that the book is done we can golf again!) Thanks to Doug Fleming, Matt Merola, Steven Soule, and Arnie Rosenthal—who all saw the spark early in my career.

And perhaps the most important motivation of all— thanks to all of you who didn't see the spark, didn't notice the potential, never spotted a hint of talent. You are the ones who motivated me every step of the way. It is you who produced my energy, passion, commitment, tenacity, fire, drive, and determination!

The Joy of Failure!

**"Only those who
dare to fail greatly
can ever achieve
greatly."**

John F. Kennedy

Let's start with the obvious—I'm going to get it right out into the open. You're probably thinking, "Is Wayne Allyn Root crazy? How could any sane person find joy in failure, rejection, adversity, tragedy, and pain? You've got to be kidding, right?"

Well, the true answer to that very natural series of questions is *no*—I am most certainly not crazy. I am resourceful, however. My unique title motivated you to buy and read this book, didn't it? It worked! I'm a motivator and you're getting motivated!

But all kidding aside, I didn't title this book *The Joy of Failure!* just for shock value or publicity. I really believe that failure is empowering. Failure is absolutely the best thing that ever happened to me. I literally failed my way to the top! In fact, it is the fear of failure and rejection that keeps most people from being successful. Let me share a true story with you, a powerful story, a story that changed my life.

A man was dying of cancer and he knew he had only days to live. He was a good man—an honest man (there aren't too many of them left in the world), a hardworking, family man. He was a loving and devoted father. But he was also a sad man because somewhere along the way, he gave up on his dreams. When his son was born, he was already thirty-five, and his son never saw him discussing goals or dreams. His life lacked enthusiasm and passion. He simply earned a living and supported a family. He had worked for almost forty years as a butcher—enduring long hours for mediocre pay. Ironically, even though he made all these sacrifices because of his children, they rarely saw him. He often left for the meat market at 3:30 A.M. and didn't return until 7:00 P.M., six days a week. He spent his whole life breaking his back for a family that he rarely saw. What a sad way to spend a life.

As his son sat by his side, watching the man dying in horrible pain, thoughts and memories came rushing to his mind. He remembered his father crying at a family gathering twenty-five years earlier. He could see the whole family gathered around him at the dining room table as he sobbed uncontrollably. He'd blocked this memory out for over twenty years, but now it was rushing back, as clear as if it happened yesterday. He decided to ask his father about it.

The man said that he had hated every moment of his job as a butcher; he felt demeaned and humiliated. But it fed his family. If he hadn't been married, he explained, he'd have quit to explore the world and find something that made him feel alive. But he had a wife and children to feed. So he felt he had no choice but to keep trudging to that same miserable little butcher shop day after day, for forty long years. He felt trapped. He actually thought of leaving his wife. But in the end, he couldn't. He stayed and sacrificed his happiness for the sake of his family—he gave up his life for his family! In every way that matters, that man died over two decades before he got to his deathbed. He made a conscious decision to give up any chance at happiness. He settled for an existence instead of a life.

As his son sobbed by his bedside, he learned just how much his father had sacrificed. He had even given up his special dream: to travel around the world. As a teenager in the navy during World War II, he had traveled the world. He loved to travel and vowed to discover new ports of call for the rest of his life. After the war, he became one of the youngest navigators in the air for Trans World Airlines. At the age of twenty-three, he was flying transatlantic flights from New York to London to Hamburg—while most of his friends had never even left Brooklyn. His son was surprised to hear that he drove a convertible sports car and was quite the dashing ladies' man. Then he married and had children, and his wife asked him to settle down for the sake of his family. So, he went to work for his father-in-law, who owned a butcher store. His wife was afraid of flying, so he only managed to get on a plane a few times for the rest of his life (all short trips). He never even got to see his son's home in California—his wife would never get on a plane for a three-thousand-mile trip. The man had the life choked out of him—he had no sparkle in his eyes. He had no interests or passions. His son had mistakenly assumed that he was always this way. But during all those painful, dreadful years the man still harbored one last dream: he dreamt that someday after retirement, he'd take a trip around the world—even if he had to spend his life savings to do it, even if he had to leave his wife behind. But someday never came. The man died of cancer, with even his one small dream unrealized.

> "You gain strength, courage and confidence by every experience in which you really stop to look fear in the face. You are able to say to yourself, 'I lived through this horror period. I can take the next thing that comes along.' You must do the thing you think you cannot do."
>
> —*Eleanor Roosevelt*

This story is especially meaningful to me because it is a personal story. It is my story. The man who died without fulfilling his dreams was my father, David Root. But my father didn't die in vain. He told me something that day on his deathbed that changed my life and led to my discovery of the joy of failure. As he lay dying, he told me he loved me, but that he feared for my future. At that very moment, I was thirty years old and already a highly paid national television sportscaster. I was living in a beautiful home on the beach in Malibu. My neighbors were movie stars and the captains of industry. I was married to the woman of my dreams—my wife Debra—and my first child was due in a few weeks. I had fought hard and made my dreams come true. Yet instead of being proud of me, my father was actually afraid for me. I was shocked and confused. But he explained, "Wayne, you've been disappointed so many times. You've had your heart broken and your head handed to you so many times. You've always had such big plans and they always seem to come crashing down. I'm so scared for you. What's going to happen to you? I don't want you to keep getting hurt—you can't keep chasing those big dreams! You are headed for a life of disappointment and pain!"

At that moment I understood why a man I thought so special, so loving, so bright, so talented had settled for a job he despised and a life of mediocrity—

> **"Life is either a daring adventure or nothing."**
>
> *Helen Keller*

because he was afraid! My father was so paralyzed by a fear of failure that he simply never tried. He was so afraid of risk that he never risked anything. He was so afraid to go for the brass ring that he wasted his life away in a butcher shop that he loathed. For his entire life he had been afraid of failing, the exact same way he was now afraid that my trying would lead to failure. He was so paralyzed by this fear that he actually thought it better to give up all his hopes and dreams. He was so blinded by this fear, that even on his deathbed he could look at my lifetime of achievements and only see the failures; so blinded by this irrational fear, that he couldn't see what all that failure had empowered me to achieve—success! I had failed so many times—but not one of them had ever frightened me or slowed me down. I just learned from them and moved forward. But my father saw me experience those same failures and he was shaken. No dream—no matter how wonderful—was to him worth the pain and failure it took to get there.

"Far better to dare mighty things, to win glorious triumphs, even though checkered by failure, than to take rank with those poor spirits who neither enjoy much nor suffer much, because they live in the gray twilight that knows not victory or defeat. The joy of living is his who has the heart to demand it."

Theodore Roosevelt

My father missed the whole point of life! Life is meant to be lived, to be experienced—not to be feared. Failure and rejection aren't bad. They are empowering! They cannot be avoided. To accomplish anything at all worth accomplishing, you've got to experience some pain along the way. To succeed, to thrive, to live the life of your dreams, you must risk failure, rejection, you must keep going. You must keep moving. You must keep fighting. That's the point of *The Joy of Failure!* That's why so many individuals never get to experience the sweet smell of success—because first you must be willing to experience the joy of failure.

Without pain, there is no gain. Without risk, there is no reward.

The ultimate irony, however, is that you can't avoid pain—certainly not by giving into the fear. Certainly not by giving up, by settling, by playing it safe. There are no shortcuts. My father was so blinded by his fear that he couldn't even see that he had endured a lifetime of never-ending pain, regret, and disappointment by not risking!

> Our deepest fear is not that we are inadequate. Our deepest fear is that we are powerful beyond measure. It is our light, not our darkness, that most frightens us. We ask ourselves, who am I to be brilliant, gorgeous, talented, and fabulous?
> Actually, who are you not to be? You are a child of God. Your playing small does not serve the world. There is nothing enlightening about shrinking, so that other people won't feel insecure around you. We are born to make manifest the glory of God that is within us. It is not just in some of us; it is in everyone. And as we let our light shine, we unconsciously give other people permission to do the same. As we are liberated from our own fear, our presence automatically liberates others.
> —Nelson Mandela (1994 Inaugural Speech)

Don't Just Survive—Thrive!

Most of the so-called experts—self-help authors, motivators, even psychiatrists—divide the human race into two distinct groups: victims and survivors. They encourage all of us to become survivors. I strongly disagree! My father was a survivor. He was a decorated war veteran, a loyal husband for over forty-five years, he raised healthy and successful children. He never borrowed money from anyone in his life. He kept a roof over our head and plenty of food on the table.

> **"Victims complain, survivors settle, THRIVERS rule the world!"**
> *Wayne Allyn Root*

Everyone in my family was patriotic and no one ever did drugs. We were a proud, law-abiding, middle-class American family. My father taught us never to complain or blame anyone else for our problems: He believed strongly in personal responsibility. By virtually any standard, my father was the very definition of a survivor. He survived life. But he never enjoyed it.

Being a survivor is certainly a step up from being a victim, but it misses the whole point of life! Where is the joy in being a survivor? It is true that survivors don't hit rock bottom, but they'll never stand on the top of the mountain at sunrise either. They live in a never-ending purgatory. They just exist. They are born, they stoically survive, then they die without making any mark on this world. They have taken the unlimited potential with which God blesses each one of us, and they have settled for a life of quiet desperation. Does this sound like success to you? Does this version of life offer you satisfaction? Is this how you choose to be remembered after your death? Is this the kind of legacy you choose to pass on to your children?

There is a third group of the human race that experts ignore: I call them THRIVERS! All the successful failures in this book are THRIVERS. THRIVERS are all about attitude. Unlike survivors, they thrive on challenge and adversity. They expect to surmount the insurmountable. They specialize in making the impossible possible. They thrive on overcoming rejection and adversity. They get high on the challenge of turning lemons into lemonade. They have boundless energy because they have a cause—they love what they are doing and they live life with gusto. They aren't afraid of risk—risk keeps them alive. It energizes and empowers them! Most of all THRIVERS never settle for anything less than the best. They are overachievers—individuals who refuse to let life control them, but instead, choose to control life. They are disciplined, committed, goal-oriented, tenacious, confident, and passionate. They are always in motion. They don't waste their lives moaning or complaining. They are dreamers, doers, leaders, and superachievers. They aim high and play to win. They don't let naysayers, cynics, or critics discourage them—the word *no* is simply not in their vocabulary. If tragedy strikes—they see it as a challenge to pick up all the pieces and put their dream back together again. You can beat a THRIVER once, twice, even three times. But you won't win the war—in the end a THRIVER finds a way to emerge victorious. They may be beaten, bloody, and exhausted, but they will find a way to stand at the top of the mountain at sunrise! That's the only group you should aim to join. Your goal should be nothing less than being the best at whatever you do.

Now, I have a few questions for you. Are you a failure? Have you ever failed miserably at something that was important to you—a job, project, career, or relationship? Have you ever let down people you loved? Have you failed a lot? Have you faced tremendous amounts of rejection, pain, and disappointment in your life? Have all these failures and rejections made you feel sad, depressed, even inferior at times? Have they caused feelings of self-doubt or self-destructive behavior? Are you tired—have all these failures and disappointments taken their toll on your mental, physical, or spiritual health? Have these failures and rejections made you afraid to take any more risks? Are you afraid to take action—to put yourself out there, to make yourself vulnerable, to put it all on the line? Is this fear of failure and rejection defining your life today? Has it made you settle for a life of mediocrity? Because of a fear of failure and rejection, have you given up on all your hopes and dreams?

That's precisely the reason why I wrote this book. I wanted you to know that failure and rejection are a natural and necessary part of the world we live in. They are experienced by everyone—even the super-rich, famous, and powerful. Even your heroes and role models. Ironically, the key to achieving success and living the life of your dreams all comes down to failure—what you do with failure, how you choose to react to it, what you learn from it. My life has been defined by failure. I am proud to call myself, "The World's Most Successful Failure"! I am a man on a passionate mission—I call it "The Root Revolution." My goal is to teach all of you how to take your challenges, failures, pain, adversity, and rejection and turn them all into extraordinary success! I want to turn individuals all over the world into "successful failures"—just like me!

I predict that your next thought will probably be something along these lines: "Come on, you're exaggerating, Wayne. Do you expect us to believe that you're a big failure?"

This question reveals a misconception prevalent in today's society—a misconception that is damaging to your psyche, your attitude, and your future progress in life. This popular misconception is that successful individuals are geniuses, who make all the correct decisions and succeed at everything they do. It's a theory that couldn't be further from the truth. You see, my road to the top was literally paved with land mines. No one—and I mean no one on earth—has found more ways to fail than me! I've been laughed at, mocked, rejected thousands of times (no exaggeration), and fired by both clients and employers. I've had hundreds of doors slammed in my face. I've had businesses fail, business ideas I thought brilliant come crashing back to earth. And then there's that infamous word, *No!* I have heard that word more times than I care to admit and it's been used against me in more imaginative ways than I knew existed: "No, you're not good enough." "No, that's not possible." "No, you can't do that—it's against the rules." "No, that idea will never work." "No, I don't want whatever you're selling." I've even heard "Don't call us, we'll call you" a few thousand times. If there is a new and innovative way to fail or to be rejected, trust me—I've already found it!

But being an admitted failure isn't so bad. I am in illustrious company. My club is populated by names I'm sure you'll instantly recognize: Sylvester Stallone, Frank Sinatra, Bruce Willis, Oprah Winfrey, Johnny

Carson, George Burns, Abraham Lincoln, Bill Clinton, Robert Dole, Steven Jobs, Donald Trump, Babe Ruth, Mickey Mantle, Dr. Norman Vincent Peale, even Dr. Seuss! The list goes on and on. Yes, those American icons are all "successful failures"—just like me! We all have the same thing in common—we failed our way to the top! Failure was the root (excuse the pun) of our personal growth and professional success. Failure motivated us and empowered us to achieve our dreams. Failure was in many ways the defining moment in our lives. Being a loser—in many cases a big loser—is what molded us into life's big winners!

I'll tell you more about these "successful failures" later in the book. But first let me tell you about me. If you're going to join "The Root Revolution," I think it's important for you to understand what I'm about and how I choose to live my life. I have a funny feeling that many of you might like to be classified by my definition of a failure! You see, I am a thirty-four-year-old, self-made millionaire. I have exceeded all the dreams I ever set for my life. I live on a sprawling, walled estate over-looking the sparkling, blue Pacific Ocean in Malibu, California. The star-studded neighbors in my exclusive, gated mountaintop community include a maharaja of India. I have been blessed with all the material things I ever dreamed of: solar-heated pool, Jacuzzi, waterfall, a state-of-the-art private home gym, even my own personal mini-golf course is under design in my backyard! And I'm not the only one who appreciates my dream estate—my home has been the backdrop for numerous movies, commercials, television shows, even a recent pay-per-view special! My home often earns money for me while I sleep! I am truly blessed.

But what is much more important than the material things are the spiritual things. Money and success are certainly a blessing—but they are not ends unto themselves. They are a means to obtain the true end—for me that end is freedom. That's what I believe life is all about—the freedom to choose and enjoy the life of your dreams! My estate includes a guest house which I have converted into my office. ROOT INTERNATIONAL—my motivational speaking firm—is run right from my home in Malibu! What that means is that I wake up in the morning to what my wife calls my "three-inch commute": I roll over from the bed to the phone on my nightstand—my satellite office. Later in the day, I'll make the longer trek to my main office—I'll walk about twenty feet to my guest house. The only traffic jam I've ever experienced is when one of my dogs is sitting in front of the door! Are you starting to get the picture? The world is full of people much richer than me, much more famous than me, much more successful than me—but few can match my lifestyle! I spend my days writing books, designing speeches and seminars, preparing for meetings, television shows, and interviews—all right in my own home, around my family—the people I love. I get to work with my wife by my side, my daughter a few feet away, my dogs at my feet, and the crashing waves of the Pacific filling the horizon. I've got the time to enjoy my family and when I'm too busy to spend any quality time with them, I can still see them a few feet away! I can take breaks when I get stressed out or burned out, play with my daughter Dakota, take a walk on the beach with my wife Debra, hike in the mountains with my dogs, swim a few laps in the pool, hit a few golf balls in my backyard, or watch one of those spectacular Malibu sunsets! I have the freedom to determine my own hours, my own income, and to decide when and where to travel. I've got no boss and no set schedule. My daughter has grown up with her father home to witness most every great moment in her young life. That's a lifestyle no amount of money can buy—it's priceless! And I thank God every waking hour of every day, for the blessings He has bestowed upon me.

So how did I achieve this wonderful life? By failing! That's right, it was failure—lots of it—that led to the extraordinary life I enjoy today. I thank God for the

> **"The things which hurt, instruct."**
>
> *Benjamin Franklin*

pain, challenges, and adversity I was able to experience so often during my journey. Failure made me tough. Failure made me wise. It made me smarter, stronger, more creative, more tenacious, more compassionate, more disciplined. Failure taught me what would work and what wouldn't. Failure taught me humility. Failure even brought me closer to God—the most important and sacred relationship in my life.

Failure taught me to treat life like "the black box" on commercial airliners. You know the black box—it's the

flight recorder on airplanes that records everything
said by the crew in the cockpit. It may be the single
most valuable piece of equipment on a
plane, because in case of a tragedy—a
crash—it will provide the only clues to
what happened and why. By studying
the last moments before a crash, investigators can put the pieces of the puz-
zle together. It may be too late for the
unfortunate victims of that specific
crash—but it isn't too late for the rest
of us. Millions of passengers fly each
year. What investigators learn from
each crash can lead to new inventions,
regulations, or guidelines that save
you or me or thousands of other flyers in the future.

> "It is impossible to
> change yesterday. It
> may be difficult to
> change today. But by
> learning from your
> past failures and
> mistakes, anything
> is possible
> tomorrow."
>
> *Wayne Allyn Root*

I've spent my adult life studying superachievers—
life's winners. They treat failure just like crash investigators treat that valuable little black box. They don't
let failure or rejection stop them or slow their progress.
They don't give up when the going gets tough. They
treat failure as a learning experience. They stay committed. They stay positive and enthusiastic. They
scratch and claw and battle. They don't complain—
they simply resolve to create the best out of the deck of
cards they are dealt!

Nothing proves my contention better than a recent
study of the top executives of the ten thousand most
successful corporations in America. Researchers looked
for a common trait for success. What they found was

astounding! Seventy percent of these movers and shakers of our society—the cream of the crop—were born and raised in the state of New York! Amazing but true! Seventy percent of the most successful leaders and doers in our great country were born and raised in the same place! Why New York? What is the significance of this amazing fact?

I believe the answer is simple: New Yorkers face failure and adversity over and over again—almost from the day they are born. Life on the mean streets of New York is cruel and unforgiving. Monumental challenges are a natural and ordinary part of life in New York. Just walking down the street is a challenge—dodging cars, crowds of pedestrians rushing to their jobs, muggers, panhandlers, street vendors, etc. Driving is a real challenge. Paying rent is certainly a challenge—two thousand dollars a month gets you a studio apartment the size of a closet, with a view of an alley. Trying to park your car is an even bigger challenge! Keeping your kids off drugs is a challenge—drug dealers blanket the city. And then there's the subway—you'll get the finger and an obscenity-laced tirade simply for making eye contact with the wrong person. But business deals in New York are the biggest challenge of all: You will face the world's biggest critics and cynics—people who root for your failure, believe nothing you say, and eat the weak for breakfast.

Do you find yourself now thinking, "What a terrible place! I'm glad I don't live there!" Well, it's actually a great place to grow up and learn about life. Frank

Sinatra said of New York, "If you can make it there, you can make it anywhere!" I'd put it differently: "If you fail enough times in New York, you can succeed anywhere else!" New York is a great training ground. It's where you learn how to fail your way to the top! Incidentally, I am proud to say I too was born and raised in New York—it's where I learned to appreciate the joy of failure!

I'm sure that you realize that not everything about New Yorkers is wonderful. Some of you are probably thinking, "Wait a minute, I can't stand New Yorkers. They're loud, pushy, obnoxious, arrogant, and self-centered. I have no interest in learning how to think like them!" Well, you're right, New Yorkers are far from perfect. Like the rest of us, they have their faults. But I'm not suggesting an either/or choice here. I think that you should adopt the best of the New York attitude and eliminate the worst.

That's precisely how my program works. To be successful, you must develop balance—a balance of spiritual and material, physical fitness and fiscal fitness. That's why the media has dubbed me a combination of a marine drill sergeant and Mother Teresa! Like New Yorkers, I know exactly what I want and I'm confident I'm going to get it. I'm aggressive, disciplined, tough as nails, full of energy, and motivated. But just as importantly, I'm also loving,

> "Fight till the death. Fight until your blood stops flowing. Until your heart stops beating. Until your lungs stop breathing. Until your cells stop multiplying. Then fight some more! All you have is your will. Your dream doesn't die, until your will does."
>
> *Wayne Allyn Root*

Successful Failures
The Root of Success is Failure!

2

"Nothing great will ever be achieved without great men and men are great only if they are determined to be so."

Charles deGaulle

One of the great myths of our media-driven society is that superachievers are better than you or me. We all read stories about the superrich and famous in *The Wall Street Journal*, *Forbes*, *Vogue*, and even the *National Enquirer*. We watch them on *Entertainment Tonight*, *Extra*, *Lifestyles of the Rich and Famous*, and E! Entertainment Television. We gape in awe at celebrities at Planet Hollywood openings. And we just assume they are different from us. We are human—flesh and blood. They must be superhuman. There's a whole industry built around that myth—publicists, public relations firms, image consultants, communications consultants, attorneys, personal assistants, and advertising agencies are all employed by the rich and powerful to exaggerate their greatness, to publicize their triumphs, and to bury their mistakes. Pretty soon we—the rest of the world who digests all this propaganda—start to believe in the infallibility, greatness, and genius of society's bold and beautiful. I call it "The Big Con"! Don't believe a word of it. The rich, famous, and powerful are the same as you and me in many ways—they need food, air, and water to survive, they bleed when cut, and they make mistakes—lots of them! The point of this book is that the one big difference between "them" and "us" is that successful people treat failure and rejection differently than the rest of us. Superachievers understand that failure is just a natural part of the process. They use failure as a learning experience. They turn rejection into a motivational tool. Successful people—even the icons of our society—fail all the time. You just rarely hear about their failures. Their eight-thousand-dollars-per-month public relations firms are paid to keep you and me in the dark. But some of our biggest stars have experienced some of the biggest flops and worst rejections of our time. Life isn't a bed of roses for superstars—or anyone else for that matter. Success isn't cheap. It takes tremendous effort, sacrifice, hard work, a lot of planning, a few crucial moments of opportunity, and a deep and personal relationship with failure!

I could write an entire book about all the famous, successful people who've failed many times in their lives. However, I'm only going to mention a few, because I want to get right on to what you can do to change your own life. It is important, however, for you to know about these successful failures, because if you begin to see your heroes as human—just like you—

capable of failing, making dumb mistakes, erring in judgment, being rejected, going through periods of dark despair, then you might be less apt to give up the next time you face adversity.

The entertainment world is full of successful failures. Arguably the greatest movie action-hero ever, this wanna-be actor couldn't even give his first screenplay away. Yet, we all know that *Rocky* went on to become one of the

> **"Experience is the name everyone gives to their mistakes."**
>
> *Oscar Wilde*

biggest hits of all time. Yes, Sylvester Stallone is today a household name. But most of us fail to remember that his follow-up to *Rocky, F.I.S.T.,* was a major flop. Or that while *Rocky* and *Rambo* have grossed over one billion dollars, Stallone has starred in a collection of box office bombs: *Rhinestone, Lock Up, Oscar, Stop or My Mom Will Shoot, Assassins,* and *Judge Dredd. Dredd* may be the most dreadful movie of Sly's career. Stallone's reward for all this failure—a new three picture, $60 million deal from MCA/Universal Pictures to start off 1996 with a bang! Is MCA/Universal crazy? Absolutely not—they simply understand the message of this book: that one success is all you need to render all your failures meaningless. People remember you for your hits—while the misses fade into obscurity. Am I wrong? Mention Stallone's name today to ten friends— ask them the first word that comes to mind. I'll wager ten to one that you'll hear "Rocky" or "Rambo." You might hear "action star," or "box office gold," or "Yo, Adrian!" But no one will say *Rhinestone* or *Stop or My*

Mom Will Shoot. Absolutely no one will say "failure." We choose to remember our heroes for their victories, not their defeats. In life, we reward those who go for the gusto and strike oil—even if it took twenty dry wells to get there!

Sly is far from the exception to the rule in Hollywood! A certain blue-eyed charmer from Hoboken, New Jersey, nicknamed "The Chairman of the Board," almost didn't get to do it his way. Frank Sinatra developed a voice problem in the early 1950s. His singing career was literally cut short due to hemorrhaged vocal cords. His acting career fared no better. His movie roles in *Double Dynamite* and *Meet Danny Wilson* were disappointing back-to-back flops. Frank Sinatra almost faded off into obscurity, just another footnote in entertainment history. But Sinatra refused to accept defeat. He took it upon himself to change the course of history. He literally begged Columbia Pictures for a role in *From Here To Eternity*. He lobbied every friend and contact in Hollywood to help him get the part. He got it! His portrayal of soldier Angelo Maggio won an Oscar, and the rest is history. Forty years, 240 albums, two thousand songs, and dozens of starring movie roles later, all the failure and adversity is forgotten. All we remember is that Frank Sinatra became the greatest popular singer of the twentieth century and a show business legend!

Overcoming rejection and failure is what show business is all about. How many of you are aware that *Baywatch* was originally dumped by NBC in 1989 after only one season on the air? *Baywatch*—just like thousands of other canceled shows—should have joined the scrap heap of television history. But in this rare case, the show's star, David Hasselhoff, decided to change history! Hasselhoff would not accept defeat. Hasselhoff and a few friends bought the rights to the show themselves and sold it to European syndicators and an American distributor. *Baywatch* had a new lease on life. Today, *Baywatch* is the most popular show in the world. It now airs in an incredible 140 countries and Hasselhoff is the highest paid actor on syndicated television.

It's not only men who experience the joy of failure. One of the most famous women in the world built her career on a foundation of failure and rejection. After losing her first job as a television anchorwoman, she switched gears and became an actress and talk show host. Her first syndicated show, *People are Talking*, made it to only thirteen cities before it was pulled off the air. But she learned from her failures. Her next talk show effort was anything but a failure. Last year, *The Oprah Winfrey Show* grossed almost $200 million! Oprah herself earned over $70 million for the second year in a row! Just the threat of her retirement recently sent syndication giant KingWorld's stock tumbling!

"Sweet are the uses of adversity."

William Shakespeare

Oprah Winfrey is a role model. She is one of the most popular women in the world. She changes people's lives and inspires viewers with her positive attitude towards life. But the only reason she is able to empower millions of others is because she stayed confident and committed in the face of failure and rejection.

Before you start accusing me of an obsession with the entertainment world, let's switch to the world of business. Does the "Lisa" sound familiar? Of course everyone has heard of Apple's Macintosh computers. But few know that Apple's first computer was a complete failure. The Lisa almost bankrupted Steven Jobs's company. But from the ashes of that terrible defeat rose the Macintosh. A few years later, Steven Jobs was forced out of the company he had founded. Ridiculed by the press and called a "has-been," he started all over again. The next decade was full of constant anguish and disappointment for Jobs. His new creation, "NeXT" Corporation, lost over $100 million, laid off half its workforce, and came close to extinction when its new personal computers were a bust. Another of Jobs's investments, Pixar, piled up huge losses. But after the release of a little film called *Toy Story* last December, Jobs achieved sweet revenge. Pixar went public and within hours Jobs's stock was worth nearly $1.5 billion. He had hit it big for the second time in his life! Computer industry critics are predicting that NeXT will be resurrected as Jobs's next home run. If they are correct, he'll have proved the critics wrong and failed his way to the top for the third time: the triple crown of failure!

> "I think and think for months and years. Ninety-nine times, the conclusion is false. The hundredth time I am right."
>
> *Albert Einstein*

Then there's Jack Welch. Welch is generally regarded as one of the best CEOs in the world. He runs General Electric. But early in his career, the plastics plant he managed for GE blew up! He was held accountable for design flaws—not a great way to start a corporate career. It takes strong personal character and a lot of tenacity to become CEO of a company after you've blown up one of it's plants. Under Welch's stewardship, GE today has the highest market capitalization of any company in the world! Welch's total compensation last year exceeded $22 million!

Failure eludes no one—no matter how big, how rich, how bright, how glamorous. It is simply a part of business. Ask "The Donald." Donald Trump—a name synonymous with wealth, success, and luxury—understands the joy of failure. Trump survived a disastrous period in the 1980s when his real estate empire crumbled, his marriage to Ivana dissolved, and his personal affairs were tabloid fodder. The picture looked pretty grim; his debt approached $5 billion. At one point The Donald was put on a monthly allowance by his creditors. He was forced to sell off many of his prized possessions—his yacht, his airline, and The Plaza Hotel. Today, Trump has left his critics in the dust with a comeback of epic proportions. His Atlantic City casinos are humming, his real estate properties once again define luxury and

> **"What do you call a businessperson who works on hundreds of multimillion dollar deals and closes only one? A millionaire—you only need one!"**
>
> *Wayne Allyn Root*

exclusivity, and even more remarkably, Trump is today virtually debt-free! That's a magic act that would make Houdini proud.

The joy of failure even extends to sports. These three men will always be remembered as baseball legends. You might remember them as prolific home run hitting champions. Their names are Babe Ruth, Mickey Mantle, and Reggie Jackson. What you may not remember is that Reggie Jackson is the all-time strike-out leader in the long history of baseball! Number two all-time is Babe Ruth! And "The Mick" is the all-time strikeout leader in the history of World Series play. These men will be long remembered for their great achievements. What is forgotten is the amount of failure and frustration they experienced along the journey! These great athletes intuitively understood that in order to succeed big, you must occasionally swing and miss! Yes, they struck out more than most, but they also hit more home runs than most! Their reward was a lifetime of fame, fortune, and adulation.

In the world of basketball, everyone knows Michael Jordan. Some believe he's the greatest player ever to step on a court. But did you know that Michael was cut from his junior high varsity basketball team? Even Michael Jordan's foundation was failure!

Troy Aikman is one of football's greatest quarter-backs. He has three Super Bowl rings to prove it! But do you remember Troy's first season with Dallas? The Cowboys won one game and lost fifteen under his leadership. He missed so much time on the field due to injuries that the press dubbed him Troy "Ache-man." To make matters worse, the man who is today a Super Bowl MVP and one of the highest-paid players in NFL history was last in passing in the entire NFL that first year!

The two biggest comeback kids of all may be the two candidates for the United States presidency in 1996— Bill Clinton and Robert Dole. Dole is the very definition of a THRIVER. He has spent his life defeating the odds—coming back when lesser men would have given up and faded away. He barely escaped death in Italy during World War II. Struck by an exploding shell, Dole's right shoulder was destroyed, the vertebrae in his neck and spine shattered, his body riddled with metal slivers. The prognosis was that he would never walk again. Dole spent three years in army hospitals— he lay in bed all that time, almost totally paralyzed. After nine major operations and a painful rehabilitation, he defied the doctors by standing, then slowly walking. His right arm was useless, forcing Dole to learn how to write left-handed. But Bob Dole wasn't satisfied with surviving—he wanted to thrive! He completed college, then graduated law school. He won election to the Kansas State Legislature, then state prosecuting attorney, the U.S. House of Representatives, and finally the U.S. Senate. But once again, even amid all that success, failure was on the horizon. Dole ran for vice president in 1976 with Gerald Ford and lost. He was blamed for the defeat. Yet in 1980, Dole was back, running in the presidential primaries and losing again.

In 1988, he was back again, running and losing again. Finally, as I write this book today, Bob Dole stands ready to accept the role he has studied for and fought for his whole life. Bob Dole is a remarkable case study of failure, tragedy, and adversity turned to extraordinary success.

But there is one major problem for Dole—standing in his way is the ultimate comeback kid. Bill Clinton's biggest failure wasn't his loss running for Congress or his defeat running for reelection as governor of Arkansas. His biggest comeback wasn't even on the campaign trail, running for president in 1992, when Clinton survived allegations of marital infidelity, drug use, and draft dodging. Yes, it was Clinton's keen understanding of the joy of failure that kept him in the race when any other sane candidate would have dropped out. Critics didn't think he'd survive any one of those charges. They called him "damaged goods." Yet Bill ignored the critics, ignored the personal character attacks, and kept on running. He brought his message to the people and asked them to decide. When the smoke cleared, Bill Clinton was left standing as president of the United States.

But Bill Clinton's biggest failure didn't come on the campaign trail. I'm referring to his performance as a speaker at the 1988 Democratic National Convention. Does anyone still remember that a young governor named Bill Clinton gave the nominating speech for Michael Dukakis? It was his big chance to impress a national television audience. He failed miserably!

Clinton was so long-winded and boring he was literally booed and catcalled off the podium. Clinton had to stop twice to ask the rude audience for quiet. The only applause came when he said, "In conclusion..." Political commentators wrote Bill Clinton's political obituary that night. Johnny Carson called him a windbag. The *Washington Post* headline read "The Numb and the Restless." Four years later that same Bill Clinton—battle-hardened by humiliation and rejection—was elected president of the United States. If you're going to fail your way to the top, the White House is not a bad place to finish!

None of my successful failures endured more adversity than Charles Schwab. Yes, that Schwab—the billionaire Wall Street discount broker! Growing up, it was Schwab's intelligence that was discounted. He could barely read or write. In college, friends had to take notes for him because he couldn't listen to a lecture and then write down what he heard. Schwab flunked French once and basic English twice! His difficulties continued in the business world when his mutual fund collapsed in 1969, leaving him over a hundred thousand dollars in debt. By 1975, however, he had come up with the idea of discounting fees for stock transactions. By 1983, his company, Charles Schwab Co., was traded publicly on the stock exchange and was valued at $425 million. Today, Charles Schwab's holdings are worth almost $1 billion! It wasn't until a few years ago that Schwab found out the source of all of his early problems—he had dyslexia!

As we end this chapter, I'd like to share one final example of failure turned to success—my personal favorite. This successful failure wasn't a politician, athlete, entrepreneur, or entertainer. He is more than just a legend. He is much more than a footnote in history. His life began amidst poverty—he was born in a manger. He would spend his brief thirty-three years experiencing every sort of failure imaginable: pain, suffering, hatred, cruelty, poverty, prejudice, persecution, and tragedy. He was ridiculed, rejected, betrayed, tortured, and finally executed for his beliefs. He never got a formal education, never owned a home—actually he was homeless—never owned a business, never had a family, never was elected to any position of authority, and never even acquired any wealth. You would think a person with that kind of track record would be long since forgotten. Yet, thousands of books have been written about him. His story has empowered and enlightened billions of human beings for almost two thousand years. No one in history has ever had a greater impact on more people. His name is Jesus Christ. Jesus Christ suffered failure, rejection, and death so that all who came after him could succeed. So in fact, the life and death of Jesus Christ is a living testament to the joy of failure!

> "Our greatest glory is not in never failing, but in rising every time we fail."
>
> *Confucius*

From Misery to Malibu
Meet The World's Most Successful Failure!

"I have not failed. I have successfully discovered 1,200 materials that won't work"

Thomas Edison (on inventing the lightbulb)

You've just been introduced to a few of the world's most successful failures. Now it's time to tell you a little about my life. If you thought the stories you just read were remarkable examples of failure turned to extraordinary success, you ain't seen nothing yet! You see, I am, without a doubt, more successful at failing than anyone who has ever walked the face of this earth. I am proud to accept the title of "The World's Most Successful Failure"! My life has been a living testament to the joy and power of failure! Some people experience the abyss once or even twice in a lifetime—sometimes it seems as if I've lived in it my whole life! Yet my life story also clearly points out that failure can be a wonderful catalyst. An educational, empowering, and life-enhancing experience. A beginning—a starting point on the road to extraordinary success!

...s in 1983. Every good story needs a
...'From Misery to Malibu!" I had just
...n college, and like most recent college
...aimless, clueless, and, for the most part,
...d no idea what I wanted to do with my life
...anted to go. No goals. No energy. No enthusiasm. ... confidence. No clue!

- **Failure number one:** In my infinite wisdom, I decided what the world needed was another lawyer. I applied for admission to law school and was promptly rejected.

- **Failure number two:** Next I decided to try my hand at real estate. I was a miserable failure and quit after six months.

- **Failure number three:** My next choice was politics. I became one of the youngest candidates ever to run for county legislator in Westchester County, New York (a suburb of New York City). I lost.

- **Failure number four:** I decided to go back into real estate. This time I opened my own firm, Wayne A. Root & Associates. I didn't sell a single property. I closed up shop within six months.

- **Failure number five:** It was here that I decided that nightlife was in my blood. I decided to raise several million dollars through my wealthy real estate contacts to purchase a famous Manhattan nightclub called Xenon. The deal fell through days before the closing.

- **Failure number six:** I determined to stay in the nightclub business and began a national advertising campaign to raise money for a chain of nightclubs in major international cities. I flew all over the country to meet with potential investors. Unfortunately none of them ever invested.

- **Failure number seven:** If nightclubs wouldn't work for me, why not try my hand at restaurants? I became manager of a hot Manhattan eatery called Danons on the Park. I did a great job—for 3 months. I got bored and quit.

- **Failure number eight:** Next brilliant decision—I decided to get into the health and fitness business. I was just starting to understand the power of a healthy diet and lifestyle. I advertised in upscale magazines nationwide. I offered to fly anywhere in the world to train clients in healthy living, eating, and thinking. I called my business From Here to Eternity. I guess you could say this was the very raw beginnings of my current program. My ads never even attracted a single call. I should have called the business From Here to Oblivion!

- **Failure number nine:** Soon thereafter, I decided to become an entertainment agent. I somehow managed to sign one client—a singer named Mark Manza. I got him one job. He fired me six months later.

- **Failure number ten:** At this point I decided to plant my feet more firmly on the ground—it was back to real estate. I was hired by the prestigious old-line Manhattan real estate firm of William B. May & Co. They were embarking on a glamorous venture—the design and marketing of a sales campaign for exclusive and exotic overseas investment opportunities. My job would require wining and dining wealthy investors all over the world. I was licensed by the SEC and NASD in the sale of tax shelters and overseas investments. Within three months the project collapsed and with it, my job!

- **Failure number eleven:** Time to flip-flop back to the glamorous field of entertainment: I opened a dating service. My matchmaking skills did not match my marketing ability. Lots of clients—very few love connections. Chuck Woolery I was not!

- **Failure number twelve:** Back to real estate again. I went to work for a commercial real estate firm in Westchester County, New York, called Bixler Real Estate. I spent over fifty thousand dollars of the firm's money creating fancy brochures and slick marketing materials. I sold absolutely nothing in one and one-half years. I was fired.

- **Failure number thirteen:** My intuitive decision-making process led to a new business—I named it Ivy League Home Cleaners. I was going to revolutionize the maid service industry by offering to homeowners clean-cut, college-educated, cleaning crews that were bonded, insured, and guaranteed to do a superior job. Great idea! Except I forgot one silly, little detail: Nobody with a college degree wants to clean toilets. I attracted lots of clients but couldn't find any employees! I failed again.

To the casual observer it would seem I was aiming for the *Guinness Book of World Records*: most failures in the shortest time, at the youngest age! The really sad part is that I was trying my best to succeed—I just wasn't very good at it! I had all the energy in the world, but I lacked focus (I didn't necessarily like anything I was doing—I just wanted to get rich), commitment (every time the going got tough, I turned tail and ran), and patience (my attention span was about ten minutes).

But it was at this juncture that a positive change in direction occurred. I had dinner with a friend and mentor, Douglas Miller, a distinguished corporate CEO. Older, wiser, and experienced at the ways of business and life, Doug took pity on me. He asked me a series of crucial questions: What did I want out of life? What were my specific goals? How would I get there? What was my game plan? It was out of this discussion at a small Chinese restaurant in Manhattan that my dream began to take shape. And it was on this night that the seeds for *The Joy of Failure!* were planted.

Doug believed that success was tied to a three-step process. Step One was simple—establish your goals.

We both agreed that my new goal was clear: to become a television sports personality. I loved sports—specifically football. I loved talking. I was a natural born communicator and I had a knack for predicting the winners of major sporting events. I would combine my talents into a lucrative and glamorous career. This goal also fit my personality. I naturally gravitated to the entertainment business. For once I was doing something that I loved—and I had a plan. That's a powerful combination! Step Two was facing the formidable obstacles that stood in my way. I was broke and had no connections, experience, or education in my field: I'd never taken a single broadcast journalism class in my life. I'd never spent five minutes in front of a television camera. And as far as connections—my father was a butcher. So if I wanted a nice piece of corned beef or bologna, I was hitting on all cylinders, but as far as knowing executive producers at major television networks, I was starting from ground zero. That brought Doug and me to Step Three: designing a game plan to overcome the seemingly insurmountable obstacles I faced. Our plan: attack, attack, and attack some more! I had no idea how much rejection and failure I was about to experience. I could have never imagined that everything I had done to this point would seem easy compared to the difficulty of the journey that lay ahead!

I started by sending out five hundred fancy brochures touting Wayne Allyn Root as the "greatest sports prognosticator in the world!" Doug and I both believed that attracting the attention of the press and building name recognition would be my best plan of attack. Five hundred brochures and press releases out, not one single response—only five hundred rejections.

So I sent out five hundred more. This time I tried follow-up phone calls. I received 499 rejections, but one bite. One small local paper in Westchester County ran a story on my budding career. They called me the new Jimmy the Greek—referring to the famous sports prognosticator on CBS television at the time.

Back to the salt mines. Photocopy the article. Type a new press release. Lick and seal. Send out five hundred copies again. No response, five hundred rejections. Try sending out five hundred more. Four hundred and ninety-nine rejections, but once again, one bite. But this time I hooked a whale: the New York *Daily News*— at the time (1986) the largest urban newspaper in America. The *Daily News* ran a full page story on "Wayne Root: The Yuppie Sports Advisor." It was the break I needed to crash through the formidable obstacles that blocked my path. And I was determined not to let it slip away. So I begged, pleaded, and cajoled fifty of my nearest and dearest friends and relatives to write laudatory letters to the *Daily News* sports editor about Wayne Root. Within a month, the phone rang. It was the *Daily News* reporter, Filip Bondy, asking for another interview. "My editor has never received so many letters about a story before. We'd like to do a follow-up story." Once again, as soon as the article was printed I went to work. Fifty more letters from friends and family were sent to the editor demanding to see more of

Wayne Root. The phone rang again—this time it was the editor offering me my own column!

Now, the description "column" would be a great exaggeration in my opinion. It was really a box—about three inches wide and four inches long. It simply contained my NFL predictions each Sunday. My pay—a whopping fifty dollars per week. It wasn't much, but it was the start I had been hoping for. It may have been a box—but it was my box and it had a byline with my name on it. And over a million New Yorkers could read it. I was in heaven!

Back to the copy machines. I made hundreds of copies of my first column, along with a press release announcing that "Wayne Root, the world's greatest sports prognosticator, is hired by America's largest newspaper." Once again, I faced hundreds of rejections, but one "yes"—NBC radio in New York. I was offered the job of predicting NFL winners on the highly rated *Joey Reynolds Show* each Friday afternoon. The pay was even worse than the New York *Daily News*—nothing! But the show offered me more exposure, more credibility and of course, the opportunity for more press releases! Once again, I was busy writing up and sending out releases with the following headline, "NY *Daily News* Prognosticator Root Joins NBC Radio." Remember that my total compensation at this point was fifty dollars per week. I was a married man living in a room in my parents' house and building mountains of debt to publicize my career. But I had high hopes, lots of energy, and tons of unbridled enthusiasm. I was in constant motion and things were happening.

My NBC press release paid off. Within a few weeks NBC Radio in Chicago called. Would I be willing to go on *The Jonathon Brandmeier Show*—the number one morning show in Chicago? This is not a tough decision. The pay isn't great—zero—but you can't beat the exposure! I've now got over a million listeners in New York, over a million in Chicago, and over a million New York readers. I'm a mini-conglomerate, yet my combined income is still fifty dollars per week! My debts are escalating—but so is my career!

I was only on NBC Chicago for a few short weeks when opportunity came knocking loudly. Radio host Jonathon Brandmeier asked me to predict the outcome of a big Monday Night Football contest between the hometown Chicago Bears and the San Francisco 49ers. When I predicted a 49ers rout, Brandmeier came to the defense of his hometown heroes, suggesting that I was being rather foolish and shortsighted "biting the hand that feeds me." He went on to suggest that the entire city of Chicago would publicly humiliate me if I was wrong. I immediately sensed an opportunity to turn this disagreement into a big event. "I'll take a chance on a public humiliation, if you will too," I responded. Brandmeier took the bait. He suggested—live on the air—that we devise a punishment for the loser of this bet. With half the city of Chicago listening, he decided that if I was wrong about his beloved Bears, I'd have to fly to Chicago to cohost his show in my underwear, outdoors, in the middle of a freezing Chicago December— in front of a crowd of thousands of screaming, taunting

Chicago fans. Now that's public humiliation. Without missing a beat, I accepted and asked him if he'd be willing to do the same. He agreed that if he lost, he'd fly to New York to host his show in his underwear, outdoors, in the freezing New York weather, with me by his side— along with crowds of hostile New Yorkers screaming and taunting him. The bet was agreed to, live on the air. My team, the 49ers, won by one of the more lopsided scores in *Monday Night Football* history, 41-0!

Brandmeier flew to New York to host his show from Rockefeller Plaza. True to his word, he stripped down to only his boxer shorts and appeared outside in ten degree weather, with me by his side. What he hadn't counted on was my turning his appearance into a major media event. I sensed an opportunity to take my career to a new level and I wasn't about to let this opportunity slide away. I emptied my bank account of my entire life savings—a grand total of two thousand dollars—and hired a major New York public relations firm to publicize the event. When Johnny B. stepped outside Rockefeller Plaza in his briefs, he was met by dozens of news organizations from around the country—UPI, AP, *Entertainment Tonight*, all the TV tabloids, newspaper photographers, television cameramen and reporters from virtually every channel in New York and Chicago, as well as several national news bureaus. I had created an event! And since it was my PR firm that was directing the event, I was the star! Headlines that night on every New York newscast sounded like this: "Chicago's biggest radio host hit town today—stripped of his pride and his clothing by famous New York prognosticator, Wayne Root!" One newscaster reported, "It's easy to tell which one is Mr. Root and which one is Mr. Brandmeier—Root is the New Yorker in the sharp suit, smiling, and looking like a winner. Brandmeier's the guy standing in the freezing cold without his clothes on!"

Overnight, I had made a name for myself! I was identified as a "winner" and a "famous New Yorker." Only hours before I was a broke nobody, living in my parents' house, working for fifty dollars per week!

Within days my phone rang. It was an executive at the NBC Source Radio Network—a group of over 125 NBC radio stations appealing to young adult listeners. A group of NBC executives had been in the audience outside Rockefeller Plaza and watched me ham it up in front of the cameras with Johnny B. One of these executives was Stephen Soule, President of NBC Source Radio. Soule liked what he saw and offered me a job as sports talk host on their 120-plus NBC stations nationwide! I was offered a fat salary and a limousine to and from work! My life had just changed forever! But my days of failing were not over by a long shot.

For several months I was limoed to and from my NBC job. In between I was whisked around the country to make publicity appearances at various NBC radio stations. I was given the star treatment wherever I went. Unfortunately, my bubble was about to burst. NBC unexpectedly announced the signing of America's Top 40 radio superstar Casey Kasem to a multimillion dollar contract. My producer hastily explained to me that those millions had to be cut elsewhere. They had decided to cut me! Easy come, easy go. I had gone from the outhouse to the penthouse and back to the outhouse again—all in a few months. But all wasn't lost— I had a unique ability to look at the bright side of things. Even though my job was axed, I still had a contract with NBC. That meant they'd have to keep paying me. And that constant source of income meant lots of money to promote my career. I was through—but I was just getting started!

I knew television was where I wanted to be, so I took my NBC income and produced a television highlight tape at a professional studio. I then acquired a list of every local television station and national cable network in America. And I began sending out tapes via Federal Express. I thought executive producers and news directors would stop and take notice of a FedEx package—I would stand out from the crowd. Unfortunately the only things that stood out were my bills for overnight shipping, copies, stationery, business cards, videos, messengers, and follow-up phone calls to all corners of the country. I was eating up my entire NBC salary and then some! My debts were growing faster than my career—much faster!

All that money I was spending wasn't even paying off. The responses I got were more than just negative—they were downright humiliating. Mostly I got "Don't call us, we'll call you." Very few producers or news directors would even come to the phone. The few that did either said, "I've seen your résumé and you didn't even graduate from broadcast school—you have no chance in this business. Stop wasting your time," or "I watched your highlight tape. It was amateurish and unprofessional. Why don't you quit before you humiliate yourself further?" It was at this time that I decided I needed a good agent. I was getting nowhere representing myself. Unfortunately my search for an agent met with more rejection. I was rejected by every agent in the sports, news, and entertainment business—no decent professional would even consider representing someone as raw and inexperienced as I was. My only choice at this point was to pose as my own agent—with his permission, I began using Doug Miller's name. The humiliations continued unabated. Out of the hundreds of rejections that I received over the next few months, one stands out above all others. I still remember it like it was yesterday. An ABC-TV producer said, and I quote: "Your client Wayne Root is a joke. This man has no talent of any kind. You should be embarrassed sending out such garbage as his highlight tape. If this isn't a joke of some kind, you should be drummed out of your profession. No professional agent would associate with this joke called Wayne Root. Hell will freeze over before this guy ever gets a job as a television sportscaster!" Looking back, this was the low point of my long journey. It was also one of many occasions when I came close to deciding to give up my dream. At this point, the odds looked more than long—they looked downright impossible.

But each time I thought of giving up, some little victory materialized that kept me going. My tapes weren't exactly lighting up the television world, but those same promotional and video materials were attracting investors. I was offered an opportunity to start a business where I'd offer my sports predictions to wealthy investors for a fee! I raised $150,000 and started a sports advisory business called Pure Profit. My goals were simple: Stay active, stay visible, keep fighting, keep moving forward. Unfortunately, Pure Profit was pure debt. Add just one more failure to the long list! No, make that two failures. As we were locking the doors and closing up shop, I was able to talk a major Wall Street underwriter into giving me a new lease on life. They agreed to raise up to a million dollars and make me one of the youngest CEOs of a publicly traded company on Wall Street. However, a small complication developed along the way to easy street—my underwriter suffered a financial setback and went out of business before the bulk of the money was raised. My company was forced out of business for the second time in a year! Pure Profit was pure debt again.

At this point, my long series of failures was beginning to take its toll. I didn't have a dime in the bank and my personal debts were approaching $150,000. It was soon after this last disaster that I was forced to declare personal bankruptcy. Within months, my first marriage was over as well—my wife announced she was leaving me for another man! I wasn't just failing— I was finding new and innovative ways to fail. And the failures seemed to be getting bigger, more expensive, and more depressing. But a thriver doesn't give up or hide under the covers. I trudged forward. Energy creates action. Action creates opportunity. Or so I hoped. And prayed!

> **"In the middle of difficulty lies opportunity."**
>
> *Albert Einstein*

Just as I hit rock bottom, I was saved again. My business may have been out of luck, my television career going nowhere, my marriage in shambles, and my bank accounts busted, but my nonstop promotions and press releases were paying off. Bantam Books, one of America's largest and most prestigious publishers, agreed to publish my first book, *Root on Risk*. It was a small and short-lived moral victory. The book was a flop—add one more failure to the long list. But being a published author opened up journalistic doors for me. The *Robb Report* magazine named me contributing sports editor. The *Robb* is like a toy store for the world's wealthiest men and women—the average reader earns almost a million dollars per year. My name was positioned in front of the movers and shakers of the business world. I was able to interview many of the biggest names in sports—Mark Spitz, Bruce Jenner, Mario Andretti, Lyle Alzado, Steve Garvey, Dallas Cowboys owner Jerry Jones, and the commissioners of the NBA, NFL, and PGA (Professional Golf Association). Despite setback after setback, I was making a name for myself, gaining credibility, and most importantly—staying in the game. I was literally failing my way to the top!

I was also attracting the attention of some major television networks. First, I was called by Bill MacPhail, the legendary boss of CNN Sports. He had an opening for a sportscaster at CNN and I was on his short list. I immediately flew to Atlanta to audition for the job. I didn't get it, but it was an honor to be considered. It gave me a boost of confidence and convinced me that my goal was indeed within reach. Within days of my return from Atlanta, Fox Television executive Michael Binkow called and invited me to fly to Los Angeles to interview for the host position of a newly proposed national television sports show. The show was aimed at a young, hip, urban audience and Binkow made it clear that I fit the bill perfectly. I was so excited and sure this was the break I'd been waiting for, I even paid for my friend and mentor Doug Miller to fly to Los Angeles with me—to act as my agent. Once I got to Los Angeles, it became clear that this was just another false alarm. The show was merely at the exploration stage. I would soon learn that in Hollywood that's television-talk for "pipe dream." But remember, at this point I was used to disappointment. I had become an expert at turning lemons into lemonade. Here I was with my "agent" in Los Angeles—all dressed up with no place to go. The trip was already paid for and I wasn't about to fly home with my tail between my legs. I decided to start "dialing for dollars." I began dialing every television station in Los Angeles. I vowed to turn a wasted cross-country trip and the biggest disappointment of my young career into the biggest break of my life—and I did!

Doug and I sat in our hotel room for two full days waiting for the phone to ring. It never did. At one point even Doug—the eternal optimist—suggested giving up and heading back home. His exact words were (we still laugh about this conversation to this day): "Wayne, it's one thing to be a positive thinker. It's another to be a glutton for punishment. You've got to know when to give up. You're humiliating yourself. Please stop—I can't stand seeing you put yourself through so much pain." Instead of listening to reason, Doug's words inspired and angered me. I made another few hours' worth of calls, and one of those calls hit pay dirt! After over a year of effort and more than a dozen calls to Arnie Rosenthal, General Manager of Financial News Network (FNN) Sports, I decided I had nothing to lose by making one more call. I was shocked when Rosenthal himself actually got on the phone. "Where are you?" he asked. When I told him I was in Los Angeles, his response was like music to my ears, "Wow, what great timing. Our number one anchorman, Todd Donoho, just announced this morning that he's leaving for ABC. How soon can you be here?" Doug and I probably set the crosstown speed record that day! Within an hour I found myself sitting in the executive offices of the Financial News Network, negotiating a deal that would put me on national television in front of over thirty-three million viewers! We shook hands that day. The official deal was negotiated by Doug over the next month. Contracts were prepared by FNN's legal

> **"Listen to your heart, not your critics."**
> *Wayne Allyn Root*

department and I signed on the bottom line—with shaking hands. Remember, I had never spent one single minute in my life in front of a television camera! I didn't know how to work a microphone, read a TelePrompTer, or edit a story. I had never even met a television sportscaster in my life! Only a few months before, an ABC producer had called me a joke, talentless, and an embarrassment to my profession.

It was now June 15, 1989. I found myself—at the age of twenty-seven—one of the youngest national television hosts and anchormen ever on a major American television network! And I had found my way to Malibu! It was a remarkable turn of events. My parents were shocked. My friends were speechless. Doug Miller was shaking his head. Even I had to pinch myself to make sure I wasn't dreaming. I had endured rejection, negativity, cynicism, and humiliation. I had stayed positive, passionate, confident, and committed in the face of insurmountable odds. I had survived divorce, bankruptcy, constant rejection, and countless failures. And here I was, on national television—a place that millions of red-blooded American sports fanatics and thousands of broadcast school graduates dream of every day. A place that local sportscasters fight and struggle for—in most cases for twenty years or more! The difference between me and them was simple—I had faith. I believed with every bone in my body that I'd make my dream come true. And I never gave up or gave in—I kept going and going and going—just like the Energizer batteries Bunny! I kept fighting, slugging, kicking, and screaming. I had found a way to smash through the obstacles, to come back again and again from adversity, to turn devastating defeat into extraordinary victory. I was bloodied and beaten, but never defeated. I lost countless battles, but I emerged from the battlefield victorious!

Whew! I'm exhausted just telling my story! I'm sure you're exhausted reading about it! But I'm not done yet. You see, it's not just struggling people who fail. Failure continues long after the struggle is over. Successful individuals—even superachievers—continue to experience failure, rejection, and disappointment throughout their lives. I was certainly no exception. But first let's take a look at the good news.

I spent 1989 and 1990 at Financial News Network—anchoring, hosting several highly rated shows, and interviewing some of the biggest names in sports. This young, raw kid who had never even met a sportscaster before, traveled the country in the summers of 1989 and 1990 with my FNN producer and videographer Petar Lasic, interviewing the biggest stars in the world of football at dozens of NFL training camps! I stood on the field next to the likes of Joe Montana, Troy Aikman, Steve Young, Jerry Rice, and Emmitt Smith. By 1990, I was writing, hosting, and producing my own special, *Athletes in Rehab.* I traveled the country discussing drug and alcohol addiction with world-class athletes. This critically acclaimed show was such a hit that it was submitted by Financial News Network for a prestigious Cable ACE award!

At one point, Jimmy "the Greek" Snyder—my boyhood idol—even came out of retirement to cohost my NFL football show on FNN. I had spent five years plotting and planning my goals (all of which revolved around replacing Jimmy the Greek), and here I was hosting a national television show with him by my side! The game plan Doug Miller and I had designed in a small Chinese restaurant had made the impossible, POSSIBLE! By 1991, I was starring in a new show, *Proline*, airing on USA Network in over 60 million cable households! I was living my dream!

But little did I realize that another long struggle was just beginning! I was about to get another strong dose of the joy of failure. You see, I'd failed my way to the top of the television broadcast business. But now I wanted to share my story with others. I wanted to become a motivator. I wanted to inspire others to reach for the stars, just like I did. I wanted to teach others that failing doesn't make you a failure. I was shocked to learn that the naysayers were out in force all over again! My motivational career was denigrated and my ideas rejected by television networks, publishers, seminar promoters, literary agents, Hollywood agents, infomercial producers, speakers' bureaus, business investors, and even other motivators. I was rejected hundreds of times, all over again. I learned a valuable lesson from this second journey to the top of my field—the odds are always against you. The naysayers will always discourage you and the battle is always long and hard no matter what your goal, no matter what your standing, no matter what your credentials. The world is full of cliques—"old boy" networks made up of those who've already made it—and they are in no hurry to admit you into their club! As a matter of fact, they will punish you, discourage you, and intimidate you every step of the way.

These painful lessons made my second journey even tougher than my first. Once again, I was subjected to such helpful and encouraging comments as: "What gives you the right to instruct others?" "Who appointed you America's success coach?" "What are your experience and credentials in this field?" "Motivational speakers are a dime a dozen. There are thousands of them—get to the back of the line." This period not only included rejections by virtually every publisher in New York and an infomercial flop—costing over $150,000 of my own funds—but the tragic and sudden death of both my mother and father to cancer—only twenty-eight days apart. It was the most difficult, trying, and depressing period of my life. My earlier struggle to reach national television seemed like a picnic in comparison!

> **"I have fought a good fight, I have finished my course. I have kept the faith."**
> *2 Timothy 4:7*

Today, all that misery seems like a lifetime ago! I am living the life of my dreams. I'm paid fifteen thousand dollars per day by major corporations to motivate and empower their executives. I am motivating and inspiring thousands of individuals at seminars from coast to coast. My audio/videotape series has been sold in all corners of the globe—to attorneys in Boston, doctors in Los Angeles, stockbrokers in New York, Amway distributors in Guatemala, and realtors in New Zealand. The national media is even joining in on the fun! The exclusive new collector's magazine, *The Trump Gift Book*, chose me as guest editor for their inaugural issue. The topic? What else? The joy of failure! The *Los Angeles Reader* dubbed me "The King of Pain"! *Entrepreneur* magazine featured my story in a section reserved for the top authors and motivators in the world! *Success* magazine chose me as one of America's top home office entrepreneurs! All of that happened in just a thirty-day period this spring! And then of course there's this book—the very one you and tens of thousands of others are reading at this very moment. All of this is possible because I never gave up, because I never listened to the naysayers, because I ignored the experts, because I had faith in God to empower me to stay strong, committed, disciplined, passionate, and motivated, because I stayed active and never stopped moving long enough to notice how insurmountable the odds really were! My dream is now a reality!

Dreams are fluid. You achieve one and you must move on to another. I am now working on a new dream—to host and produce a television show called *Success 101*—a talk show that speaks to today's younger generation. *Success 101* will teach young adults—high school students, college students, and Generation Xers just joining the workforce—what success is all about in the real world. I want to teach young adults what nobody ever bothered to teach me—not the three R's (Reading, 'Riting, and 'Rithmetic), but rather the ABCs of success! I want to prepare our next generation of leaders for the reality that failure, rejection, and challenge are a natural part of the learning process. I want to empower them with the understanding that success is all about overcoming the fears and the obstacles. That you don't surmount the insurmountable with your head (education from a book), but rather with your heart, your spirit, and your will.

> **"What is the point of showing kids the best cars, clothes, homes, stereo systems, vacations—if you don't empower them with a knowledge of how to acquire them?"**
>
> *Wayne Allyn Root*

I want to empower and enlighten young people with the most valuable course of their lives—Success 101. I only wish that when I was young and impressionable, someone had been there for me. I could have avoided a tremendous amount of pain and disappointment. Today, I want to be there for a new generation—this is my passion, this is now my calling!

Ironically, things worked out for the best for me. I believe we all have a purpose in life, that we are all part of a grand plan. I can see now that I needed to experience all that adversity so that I could pass my lessons on to others. My story empowers others because I had to live every painful minute of it, because I was willing to risk, to fail, to stick my neck on the chopping block—to experience pain and humiliation.

e rejection and failure are forgotten;
llion miles away. I've come a long way
n, New York. I've come a long way from
r-per-week salary. I've come a long
ainful bankruptcy. I've come a long way
being laughed at and called a joke! Yet I can never
forget all those lessons; they will be forever a part of
me. They molded my character. They made me the person I am today. No matter how successful I become, the
root of my success will always be failure.

For those of you experiencing pain at this moment,
I ask you to be kind to yourself. Be patient. Be tenacious. Stay committed to your dreams. Have faith in
your power to overcome the obstacles that block your
path. Learn from the pain and the failure.
Understand that it's all worth it—all the pain, all the
humiliation, all the sacrifice. You've got to fight for
anything worth having, and success is worth having!
Once you've climbed your mountain, the pain and
rejection will seem so small, so unimportant, so far
away. Yes, when I look back, it was all worth it—and
then some.

Ecstasy is the other side of pain! That's the feeling
you're looking for. You can't find it hiding under the
covers. You can't find it sitting on a sofa, watching a
soap opera. You can't find it smoking dope or getting
drunk. You can't find it by accepting mediocrity—by
settling for a life of no risk, no adventure, no passion.

You can only get it by letting go of your fears—by risking, by dreaming, by fighting, by failing—until you hear that one single, solitary, magical, mystical, empowering *yes!* that will change your life!

"Never, never, never quit."

Winston Churchill

Building Your Foundation

> **"Impossibilities vanish when a man and his God confront a mountain."**
>
> *Rev. Robert Schuller*

I n the next chapter, I'm going to start giving you specific instructions on how you can change your life, how you can build on your failures, how you can prepare, think, look, and act to turn failure into success. But before you start building your new life, you need to make sure that its foundations are sturdy. You need to be in the right mindset before you can take on the world and create the life of your dreams.

Faith

I have a confession to make. Even though I strongly believe in the power of principles like passion, energy, enthusiasm, confidence, and tenacity, I must admit that it's all meaningless and powerless without God. A faith in God is my anchor—the root of my passion, my energy, my tenacity. God is my base—the foundation of all I do and all I am. I devote my life to God and it is from him that all my ideas spring forth. I credit every word in *The Joy of Failure!* to God. God inspires me. God challenges me. God motivates me. God fills me with love. God gives me hope. God is who gives me energy, passion, enthusiasm, and confidence. God is the reason you are reading my words at this very moment—God led me to motivate and empower you. God led you to me—to be motivated and empowered. There is nothing and no one in my life more important than my faith in God.

> "Faith is to believe what we do not see and the reward of this faith is to see what we believe."
>
> *St. Augustine*

What exactly is faith? When I talk about faith, I am referring to a deep and abiding confidence in the existence of something that inspires you, something loving and powerful. For me, that something is God.

It has been my experience that individuals with faith are less lonely, happier, healthier, more positive, more loving, more fulfilled, even more successful. The most miraculous changes in my life didn't develop until I developed a faith in God. My life changed, my attitude changed—the way I viewed life changed—in dramatic fashion on the day I developed a close, personal relationship with God. I tapped into feelings and emotions I hadn't even known existed—love, compassion, respect, commitment, dignity, integrity, forgiveness, charity. On that day, a whole new world opened up to me!

Why did a faith in God change my life? First and foremost, God inspires me to do all the things THRIVERS must do. God inspires me to believe in miracles—to aim high, to make the impossible possible. God inspires me to move mountains, to overcome insurmountable obstacles, to do things others say cannot be done. To ignore the limitations set by the naysayers—to create my own realities. God inspires me to do great things, create great things, feel great things, and think great ideas. And perhaps most importantly, God inspires me to share my ideas with others—it is God who encourages me as an author, speaker, motivator, and positive thinker.

Second, there is no more powerful concept in life than teamwork. No person is an island. We are all human—we all need help, advice, love, strength, and friendship. God is the ultimate teammate—with him by my side I am unbeatable. Having God in your life is the very definition of confidence! If two heads are better than one, having God as a partner is like multiplying your strength by one hundred million! Alone, many things are just not possible, but with God by your side—guiding you down the right path—anything is possible!

Third, a faith in God reduces stress and fear—the two biggest obstacles to building the life of your dreams. Prayer acts as a safety valve. At the very moment you speak to God about the burdens, doubts, and fears in your life, they are instantly released—like pressure in a valve. Stress is greatly reduced or eliminated. Without stress and fear blocking your creativity, you are free to intensely focus on the things in life that matter to you—empowering you to be a better spouse, parent, employee, boss, or human being! You are able to express your creativity in ways you never knew existed—making you more valuable to all around you and enabling you to earn more money than ever before. Yes, spiritual wealth even leads to material wealth! That's the power of faith and prayer at work!

Fourth, God keeps me honest and moral. In a world fast decaying all around us, it is moral weakness that seems to be at the root of our destruction. With God as my partner, I act the way I think God wants me to act, I do what I think God would do. I treat others the way I'd like to be treated. And when I'm feeling weak and under stress, I turn to prayer instead of drugs, alcohol, and other self-destructive behavior to get me back on track. Fifth, prayer energizes me. It infuses me with energy, enthusiasm, and passion. And with qualities like those, I am unbeatable and unstoppable. Failure, fear, and rejection are powerless when faced with this kind of supercharged, supermotivated, superenergized attitude. Because of my faith in God, I am committed to my goals and dreams for the long haul—no matter who or what stands in my way!

And finally, prayer is the highest possible form of positive thinking because of the powerful mindset it creates. When I pray, my problems become meaningless and minuscule. No matter what my mood, no matter how down I was when I began, prayer lifts my mood and supercharges my spirits. It is the most powerful way I know of to create a positive attitude—it works in any situation instantly. Prayer is a miracle in itself!

So this is my foundation: All else I do and believe is built upon faith. God has blessed me, turned my life around. He can do the same for you! In an age of cynicism and negativity, this may not be a popular message—but it is my message. It is my starting point for all that I do, and most importantly, it is the truth!

So here's the answer to your first *how?*—How do I stay positive? With faith and prayer. How do I stay motivated? With faith and prayer. How do I stay confident? With faith and prayer. How do I stay committed to my goals? With faith and prayer. How do I turn failure and rejection into extraordinary success? With faith and prayer!

Family

A faith in God and family go hand in hand, like peanut butter and jelly. My dependence on family started early in life. My mother and father may not have been multimillionaires or superachievers, but they were great parents. They built a base of love that kept me strong when facing adversity. When they were both stricken by cancer, my wife became my anchor. Within two weeks of their death, my daughter Dakota was born. It was a time of endings and beginnings. Their deaths were traumatic, yet my daughter's birth was a dramatic symbol of renewal—a true gift from God. Again and again when facing adversity, challenge, even tragedy, I have been blessed with the innate sense to choose family—instead of negative

> **"Woman knows what man has too long forgotten, that the ultimate economic and spiritual unit of any civilization is still the family."**
>
> *Clare Boothe Luce*

choices that could have, at worst, ruined my life or at best, deepened my despair.

To prove my point, I have to look no further than the town I call home—Los Angeles. Wealth and power are the twin gods of Los Angeles. The dream here does not include faith or family—in Hollywood, excess is the norm. Goals here revolve around bank accounts so big you could never spend all the money in ten lifetimes; homes so big you'd need a walkie-talkie to communicate with your spouse; weekend jaunts to Paris or Monte Carlo; and spending sprees on Rodeo Drive that surpass the gross national product of Liechtenstein. That's the definition of success around here! Money, power, and sex are what it's all about.

A popular Los Angeles entertainment industry joke sums up life in La-La Land: A successful actor returns from a long day of meetings and interviews in Hollywood. As he nears his opulent mansion, he notices a cloud of smoke. The closer he gets, the nearer the smoke. As he pulls up to his driveway, he realizes it is his house on fire. He is horrified to see an army of fire trucks and ambulances surrounding the burning rubble of his former home. As he races from his Ferrari, he is met by the fire chief.

"I'm so sorry sir. We did all we could," says the distraught fire chief. "Your agent stopped by this morning and saw smoke. But by the time he called us it was too late. Your wife, children, maid, nanny, cook—all gone. Your house is rubble. It's all gone—I'm so sorry."

The famous actor replies, "Wait a minute. Did you say my agent stopped by?"

The point of the joke, of course, is that the famous actor is more concerned about his career than the death of his family. An exaggerated attempt to describe life in the big city? Perhaps. But not as far from the truth as you might suspect.

I remember back to my first few years in Los Angeles. I managed to sign with a high-powered agent in Beverly Hills. When I informed him I was about to get married, his response was interesting to say the least. "I want to give you some advice," he began. "Marriage is not a joke. You've got to take this commitment seriously. Too often young people today get married without even a rudimentary understanding of the consequences. This girl could take everything you've got! Do you understand that? Everything! I hope you've protected your assets. Anything you can't protect—hide! And by the way, who's drawing up your prenuptial? I have a great attorney!"

I couldn't help but laugh. This—in all seriousness—was my agent's sincere attempt at instilling me with moral values—Hollywood style. I thought I'd just experienced the height of cynicism—until two days later, in the office of a successful television producer.

"It's nice to see someone still believes in marriage," he began. "Great institution. Let me give you some advice—give this girl your full attention. Take her seriously. Treat her well. Remember, for better or worse, you're going to be spending the next ten years of your life with her!"

"Ten years?" I replied. "Don't you mean the rest of my life?"

"Wayne, let's get serious. This is Los Angeles! Ten years is a lifetime!"

So much for family values and loyalty in Tinseltown. Why is family so important? And is it possible to place a strong emphasis on family without damaging your career? Two recent studies may surprise you.

A study of five thousand men and women over the course of two decades (starting in the early 1970s) came to a startling conclusion—those who placed a higher priority on family than career, almost twenty years later were both happier and wealthier! That's right—the family-oriented individuals had higher self-esteem and personal satisfaction levels, larger incomes, and had moved further up the career ladder than those who stressed career and wealth! So in addition to a happier life, an emphasis on family leads to a wealthier life as well!

A second study of nine thousand corporate executives over a ten-year period yielded similar results. After analyzing reams of information about a group that society would define as successful, researchers isolated one pattern above all else: ambition, drive, perfectionism, and a lust for power actually makes you sick! They found that an obsession with your career leads to higher rates of stress, illness, and disease.

> "As are families, so is society. If well-ordered, well-instructed, and well-governed, they are the springs from which go forth the streams of national greatness and prosperity—of civil order and public happiness."
>
> *Thayer*

What do these dramatic results mean? Is success really bad for you? Well, first of all, let me explain that I enjoy wealth and all its trappings. There is nothing wrong with money, power, or success. My success has put my family in a well-built house in a safe, guard-gated neighborhood. My success puts the people I love in a well-built car, with new tires and brakes. My success pays for the best education for my daughter, Dakota, and it guarantees she can go to any college she chooses someday. My success guarantees her the best health insurance and in the case of illness, the best doctors. My success affords us the ability to eat organic foods, grown or raised without chemicals, pesticides, or drugs. My success means my family doesn't have to worry about putting food on the table or paying for the mortgage. My success has allowed me to build a career at home, where I can spend more quality time around my family. What could possibly be bad about wealth or success? Who wouldn't want to guarantee the best life has to offer for their family?

Most of you are reading this book because you want to learn more about success, wealth, and power. You want to motivate and empower yourself to provide your loved ones with the best life has to offer. Many of you might have bought a motivational book like mine, thinking that Wayne Root is all about wealth and power. I am. Yet I've reached the same conclusions as the authors of those two powerful studies: wealth, fame, and power are best achieved by placing your emphasis on God, faith, and family!

Most peoples' thinking about the purpose of life is all backward. Lasting success has nothing to do with money. It has to do with health, happiness, and satisfaction. It has to do with the people we love. It has to do with how you feel at the end of the day. It has to do with how many lives you've touched. It has to do with how you'll be remembered long after you die. It has to do with balance—a synergy of ambition, drive, and tenacity, welded to love, compassion, and integrity. Wealth is simply a by-product of a life lived with passion and purpose. Wealth cannot buy you health or happiness or the love of your family. But—as those studies prove—an emphasis on family can buy you a better job, title, and income!

> "Fellow citizens, why do you turn and scrape every stone to gather wealth and take so little care of your children, to whom one day you must relinquish it all."
>
> *Socrates*

How does family translate to the bottom line? Think about your goals and aspirations. What are your choices in life? You wouldn't choose to spend the rest of your life with a corporation, a business, or an office. You wouldn't choose to spend the rest of your life with your boss, office manager, or business partner. You wouldn't choose to define your purpose in life as a salesperson, entrepreneur, or corporate executive. Is that how you'd like to be remembered by friends and family—he gave his life to his company? Is that how you would like to define your life on your deathbed? He or she was a salesperson above all else. I hope not.

You did, however, choose to commit the rest of your life to your spouse. You did choose to have children. They are your legacy—they are part of you—not your company or business. Your blood flows in their blood. They are your responsibility. And if you spend time with them, teach them well, and shower them with love, they will return that commitment with unconditional love for the rest of your life. They are the ones who will be there as you take your last breath. They are the ones who will remember you long after you are gone.

> **"The man who lives for himself is a failure... the man who lives for others has achieved true success."**
>
> *Norman Vincent Peale*

Now think for a moment about your life—about our priorities in today's modern society. Why do so many of us choose to spend most of our days at an office or business—away from the people we love, away from the people we are committed to spending our lives with? Is something wrong here? We spend only a small portion of our day with the people who love and nourish us, while we choose to spend a majority of our waking hours with those who add little to our lives.

It's no wonder those who spend more time at the office are sicker. It's no wonder those driven by career alone die of illness and disease. It's no wonder those who place emphasis on work feel less satisfaction. And it's clear why an emphasis on family leads to more money and a healthier career—people who are happy, stay healthy. Healthy people make better decisions under pressure. Healthy people can produce more in less time—they can produce more in five hours than a workaholic can in a fourteen-hour day. Healthier people are more focused. They are more positive. They have more energy, passion, and enthusiasm. They are more creative. Most importantly, if overcoming failure and rejection is the key to success—healthier, happier individuals are better able to recover from failure and rejection. Healthy individuals are better equipped to face challenges and overcome obstacles.

Yes, family does add up to a healthier bottom line—as well as a healthier life. Money, wealth, and power are all wonderful. I believe we are all meant to share in the abundance of this universe. God wants all of us to be rich. But all the riches in the world are worthless without someone to share them with!

So once again, I answer that all-important question, "How?" How do I stay motivated, even in the face of adversity? How do I stay positive, even in the face of great personal and professional challenge? How do I stay calm when facing deadlines and important business decisions? How do I recover from devastating failures and disappointments? The answer is simple: I turn to my family!

Freedom

Freedom is my way of describing what I believe will be the business phenomenon of the twenty-first century: combining career and family with a home-based business. Professionals and entrepreneurs of all kinds—

lawyers, doctors, psychiatrists, consultants, architects, computer experts, salespeople—no longer need to work in an office. With the advent of computers, modems, satellite dishes, portable computers, faxes, cellular phones, pagers, e-mail, the Internet, and voice mail, almost anyone can handle a job or run a business from home. Entire businesses are being created to capitalize on this phenomenon—multi-level marketing companies are grossing billions of dollars annually in all corners of the world. Even big business is getting into the act by encouraging employees to telecommute or work four-day workweeks. At this moment, over 27 million full or part-time businesses are run out of the home in America. Another 12 million Americans do at least some office work at home. And over 8 million employees telecommute for large corporations. That's a grand total of 47 million home office devotees! That's almost one-fifth of the entire population of America! By the turn of the century those numbers will escalate dramatically—not just in America, but all over the globe!

The home office trend is growing so fast that real estate developers are looking to take advantage. Developers in Maryland are building shopping centers with retail stores downstairs and shopkeeper's living quarters above. Developers in Toronto are building single-family homes with huge home offices already built into lofts or basements, wired with high speed fiber-optic lines

> **"There's no place like home. There's no place like home. There's no place like home."**
>
> *Dorothy from*
> The Wizard of Oz

for sophisticated computer and Internet capability. And developers in California are building apartment complexes—not only wired for business—but with a centralized communications center, complete with meeting rooms and teleconference capabilities. The differences between home and office are fast becoming blurred.

I believe that working at home is the solution to many of society's biggest problems:

- Individuals who work at home get to spend more time with their families.

- Less commuting means less stress. Less stress means a healthier, more positive outlook on life—which often translates to a more successful career and family life. Less stress means lower doctor bills and lower health insurance rates. Less stress also translates to a longer, more productive life—more time to spend with the people you love, doing the things you love!

- Less commuting means more time to devote to a wide choice of endeavors—family, education (perhaps a master's degree?), golf, a second business, more vacations—the list is endless. Study after study proves that in the stressful decade of the 1990s, time—not money—is the number one commodity. Working at home gives you the opportunity and the extra time to live your life to its fullest.

- Less commuting means less gas, oil, and wear and tear on your car, fewer accidents, lower car insurance rates, less pollution and wasted resources for our planet. Now that's what I call a valuable bonus—leaving a cleaner, healthier world for our children.

• Less commuting translates to less time in traffic jams and more time to nourish your body, mind, and spirit. The time you previously spent in bumper-to-bumper traffic, you can now spend on the treadmill or bike, meditating, praying, or exercising your mind on a new book. With all that extra time you've now freed up, you'll no longer have to gulp down a soda, cheeseburger, and fries at that fast-food joint—you'll have the luxury of being able to prepare and enjoy a leisurely, healthy, home-cooked meal.

• Building a home-based business means no boss, no limits to your income, the ability to choose your own hours and determine your own vacation time.

We are blessed to live in a day and time where you can do virtually anything right from your own home. I get haircuts at home—my stylist comes to my home once a month, where she cuts my hair poolside; I get massages at home—my masseuse makes house calls with his own massage table; I don't belong to a gym—I work out at my own personalized home gym; I don't need to go grocery shopping—my local health food supermarket, P.C. Greens, takes my order via fax and delivers within the hour! I vote at home—like millions of Americans, I don't have to leave my home to vote! At many voting precincts around the country, absentee ballots represent 50 percent of all votes. My four-year-old daughter even takes computer lessons at home—she can travel the world on the Internet, without leaving my sight!

The newest trend is the ability to further your education at home! I got a master's degree and a Ph.D. right from the privacy of my own home. Anyone can broaden their educational qualifications, further their career, and gain credibility by studying for an advanced degree through accredited home study courses, telecourses, or by taking classes on the Internet! There's a whole new world out here for you to explore—the irony is that you can do more and travel farther than ever before—without leaving the comfort of your home! You can do it all in a silk robe, from a desk in your bedroom.

It's obvious why working at home or building a business at home is the ideal career choice for the twenty-first century. Millions are opting out of the office rat race every year. Not surprisingly, their new lifestyle revolves around faith and family. Work is no longer a burden if you can do it around the people who love, nourish, and nurture you! Another big bonus is the opportunity to work in a place that nourishes you. You chose your home—you bought it because it nourishes your spirit. You decorated it with furniture, plants, artwork, books, flowers, and even electronic equipment that makes you happy—that reflects your personality.

> **"Home is the place where, when you go there, they have to take you in."**
>
> *Robert Frost*

Your home is your castle—it moves you, it energizes you, it motivates you. Why should you be away from it all day? Why should you be forced to spend most of your day in a drab, confining office—breathing stale uncirculated air, under harsh, fluorescent lights? Why spend your day around people you don't like? Who decided you should work eight to ten hours per day? And why 9:00 A.M. to 5:00 P.M.—what if those are not your most productive hours?

The catch phrase for the 1990s is "personal responsibility." Building a home-based business is the ultimate example of personal responsibility. You now answer only to yourself. You decide your hours. You decide when you will take a vacation. You decide when to leave work early or stay late. You decide if your child needs your undivided attention for a few hours in the middle of the day. You decide if you deserve a day off to play golf. You decide how to spend the time you've saved by not commuting. It's called freedom. It's wonderful. I thank God every day for this blessing He has bestowed upon me. I believe it is the ideal way to arrange life and career as we approach the new millennium.

Many of you may not be able to build a home office or home-based business today, but you can certainly set a goal and design a game plan to be working out of your home—and enjoying the life of your dreams—in the next five or ten years! Remember, with the right attitude, anything is possible.

Once again, I've answered a "How" question: How do I stay motivated? It's easy to stay positive, motivated, and committed when I'm in an environment specifically created to feed and nurture my body, mind, and spirit. It's easy to focus on my goals and be creative when I'm able to exercise, pray, meditate, and go for a swim anytime I choose. It's easy to keep my energy high and my spirits elevated when I'm able to conduct business sitting poolside in the sunshine on a beautiful Malibu day. It's easy to reduce fear when I'm able to work with my wife and daughter only steps away and my dogs at my feet. It's easy to avoid burnout when I can choose to vacation as often as I need to. It's easy to stay healthy when I have the time to exercise and eat right.

The most important point of all is that I am not special. You can enjoy all these same blessings. Simply start practicing the first step of my powerful program—faith, family, and freedom. That's HOW to change your life and start building the life of your dreams!

Designing the Life of Your Dreams

Doing It with Power Principles and Positive Addictions!

"Successful individuals not only learn from the mistakes of others, they also learn from the success of others."

Wayne Allyn Root

Introduction

Now comes the meat and potatoes of my book—the part most other motivational gurus leave out. The "how to" part of motivation—How do you get motivated? How do you thrive in the face of adversity? How do you overcome insurmountable odds? How do you stay positive when facing massive rejection? How do you stay energized, enthusiastic, passionate, and committed every day? How do you pick up the pieces when your life is in shambles? How do you turn the damaging word *no* into the empowering word *yes*?

I recently read one of the most inspiring books of our time. It's called *Chicken Soup for the Soul*. It's compelling, awe-inspiring, compassionate, and entertaining—all rolled into one. I loved it. If you want to be inspired, read it! *Chicken Soup* is indeed good for you,

missing the main course. Like most moti-
s, it is just an appetizer. It never provides
urse, real solutions to real problems.

one will make you feel better for a few
moments—like chicken soup when you're sick—but it
won't change your life. You can't thrive on a steady diet
of chicken soup. You also need a main dish—the meat
and potatoes.

Like *Chicken Soup*, this book is meant to be inspiring. But *The Joy of Failure!* does more than just talk
about inspiration—it empowers readers to change their
luck and their lives! My program teaches you how to go
out and do it! It's like meat and potatoes for the body,
mind, soul, and wallet! This program is revolutionary
simply because it's real—it isn't just philosophy that
sounds nice in a book or soothing, lovey-dovey, New Age
fluff. It changed my life—now it's time to change yours!

The program is simple. Once you've built a strong
foundation of faith, family, and freedom, you need to
understand, master, and put to work certain principles
and truisms of life that I call Power Principles. Then
you need to change some of the habits of your life. In
fact, you need to become "addicted" to good habits. I
call these Positive Addictions. These two—Power
Principles and Positive Addictions—are all you need.
And they're simple! You can start today!

POWER PRINCIPLES

Are you afraid that you're missing some magical or
mystical quality that you need to succeed? Are you

putting off starting your new life because you don't believe you have what it takes? Knowing how to succeed is a skill that you can learn, just like you learned to drive an automobile or read a book. You and I weren't born with the ability to fend for ourselves. We couldn't make our own meals. We couldn't change our own diapers. We couldn't feed ourselves or dress ourselves. We couldn't even talk at birth. We certainly were not born with an understanding of reading, writing, or arithmetic! How did we learn? Someone had to show us how. And we copied—we emulated whatever they did. So in fact, the process of education—acquiring knowledge—is simply watching what others do and copying it for ourselves!

Success is no different. Most of us really don't understand the process of success. We've been taught little or nothing about it our whole lives. What little we've been told is erroneous. We've been told that success is a deep, dark, complicated, and burdensome process. It's a big secret and if we are not part of the privileged few who know the secret, we're out of luck. Many of us believe success is something off-limits—it's sort of an exclusive club reserved for others.

Well, I'm here to simplify the process. Success is not complicated. It isn't a deep, dark secret. It isn't reserved for a special few. Success is an acquired skill. Just like reading, writing, or arithmetic, it can be taught. You can learn how to do it—by emulating others. Successful individuals—THRIVERS—are not born, they are made. Anyone can be successful. You just have to find someone who is already successful and willing to teach you.

> "As I grow older, I pay less attention to what men say. I just watch what they do."
>
> *Andrew Carnegie*

Let me tell you a wonderful story about the process of success. This story was passed on to me by Pastor Dave Owen of the Malibu Vineyard Church. It is a great illustration of human nature and why we do the things we do!

Each Christmas for a decade, a man attended the same family Christmas dinner. They were a wonderful, loving family and the wife who cooked Christmas dinner each year was a charming hostess. But one thing bothered this man. Actually it was more than a bother—it drove him crazy! Each year he watched his hostess cut the tail off the ham before putting it in the oven! And every single year he asked her the same question—why? Her answer was always the same—"Because that's the way my mom did it." That answer just seemed silly to this wise man—it just didn't make sense to him. He kept thinking, "But why did your mother do it that way?"

Finally, one year the mother of the hostess came to Christmas dinner. The man couldn't resist this opportunity to finally get an answer to his question. He cornered the mother and asked the question that had been bothering him for a decade. "Your daughter says she cuts the tail off the ham before putting it in the oven, because that's the way you always did it. So please tell me: Why did you do it?"

The mom's answer was simple: "Because my pan was too small and we were too poor to afford a bigger pan."

Doesn't that sum up the riddle of success? Most of us go through life believing and doing and emulating whatever we watched our role models do—our parents, grandparents, friends, and teachers. Even worse—like that hostess who always cut the tail off the ham—we copy these traits and habits without questioning if they are right or wrong, without questioning if they are still valid today, without questioning if they apply to our lives, without questioning if they are positive or negative to our future success and well-being.

What if the habits, traits, and attitudes you learned from your parents were unhealthy? What if what you learned as a child will stifle your progress as an adult? What if the ideas and beliefs you learned hanging out on the street corner with your friends were born of ignorance? What if practicing these habits impedes your growth?

> **"Can a blind man lead a blind man? Will they not both fall into a pit? A student is not above his teacher, but everyone who is fully trained will be like his teacher."**
>
> *Luke 6:38*

Unfortunately most of us go through life copying the wrong people. If our parents or friends were unsuccessful financially, spiritually, or emotionally, we tend to follow the same patterns. There is a distinct pattern in the lives of most families—generation after generation makes the same mistakes and suffers the same failures. But it doesn't have to be this way. Each of us has the ability to start a new pattern—a healthy, successful pattern. There is a formula for success: a pattern successful people follow. People like this are emotionally stable. They enjoy rich spiritual lives. They are healthy and active. They have a positive self-image. They choose to respond to challenge and adversity in a positive, healthy way. They are not self-destructive—they do not choose to destroy their success. They have a passion for life. They love what they do. They actually look forward to getting up in the morning and facing life. They are THRIVERS! They enjoy the respect of their peers—they are regarded as the best at what they do. They are among the lucky few who enjoy the life the rest of us dream about! But luck actually had nothing to do with it—in each and every case, what made THRIVERS so special was their ability to visualize the life of their dreams, plan it out, then go out and make it happen!

The good news is that THRIVERS aren't born special. But they have learned to be special. The even better news is that you can learn to be special too! You've just got to live life by the same principles as they do! The best news of all, is that I've isolated the principles that make a person special, powerful, and successful. I call them Power Principles. And I'm going to share them with you! But first you must learn a valuable lesson from that hostess on Christmas night, who chose to blindly emulate her mother—if you're going to copy the habits of others, be sure to choose a habit worth copying! Actively choose to copy the successful habits and principles of life's winners—THRIVERS!

POSITIVE ADDICTIONS

The attributes and skills necessary to succeed at life are much like those necessary to succeed at sports. A great athlete speeds up by slowing down. Magic Johnson leads a fast break so naturally, because he can do something most of us cannot—he can slow down his field of vision, so that everything seems to move in slow motion. You and I see ten players racing downcourt at breakneck speeds. We get so confused, we can't make a decision at all—let alone a good decision. But Magic has the ability to clearly focus on one particular target—in slow motion. By slowing down the action, he is able to make passes behind his back, through his legs, right past stunned and embarrassed opponents. Magic's opponents see things at normal speed while he has seen it all in slow motion. It's all oh-so-easy when you slow it down!

Baseball works the same way. The great hitters are able to hit a tiny baseball traveling at over ninety miles per hour, while it is spinning, curving, and dipping! How do they do it? They can do something you and I can't. They can slow down their field of vision. The great hitters of our time don't see a tiny dart moving at ninety plus miles per hour. They see a watermelon moving in slow motion! Hitting a home run when you're in a groove is easy. Everything is larger and slower than real life!

Let's look at auto racing—a favorite sport of mine. Do you think great race car drivers win races because they are faster than their competition? Do you think it's all about speed? Speed actually has very little to do with winning auto races! Great race car drivers must be great athletes and great thinkers. There are literally dozens of things going on at once—all at two hundred miles per hour. Racing is all about concentration and focus. The goal is not driving faster, but deciding faster—making crucial decisions under intense stress and pressure. How intense? Heat within the car reaches well over one hundred degrees. Simply gripping the steering wheel is equal to squeezing twenty pounds of force eight hundred times during a race! Add to all this stress the fact that one split-second lapse of concentration could result in serious injury or death for the driver. Whew! What a way to make a living—pure macho adrenaline rush! But the key to success on the racetrack is not macho speed, but slowing down your mind. A race driver must calmly see all his or her gauges, the track, the ever-present wall, and all the other drivers—all at split-second intervals, traveling at speeds of two hundred miles per hour or faster. Success is all about seeing the whole field in slow motion. One mistake or lapse and your opponent could maneuver by you. Once you relinquish the lead, it's almost impossible to catch up. Mistakes are intolerable. Ironically, if a race car driver is successful at slowing his field of vision down, he or she will automatically race faster and more efficiently.

Success at anything in life is no different. You must slow down in order to clearly hear your own inner voice—your intuition. You must slow down to tune into your own natural wisdom. You must slow down to clearly see the field in front of you. You must slow down to listen to what's happening around you. You must see life in slow motion as you make critical decisions—just as a point guard, a baseball player, or a race car driver slows down to make critical decisions! You must slow down your field of vision in order to live life in the fast lane.

The way to slow down, to give yourself the time you need to make good decisions, is the same way that athletes do it: you practice good habits until you can perform at your peak naturally—without even thinking about it! You become so fanatical in your devotion to developing these habits that they're more like addictions. For instance, if you've trained yourself to be sensitive to and aware of the body language of other people in a meeting you will automatically pick up and understand what is being communicated nonverbally without even thinking about it. Instead of trying to understand "where they're at," you'll already know where they're at and can be mentally plotting strategy that takes this information into account. Positive Addictions isn't a program—it's a lifestyle—a way of living. It's a way of succeeding at life by making healthy habits a natural part of your life.

FIVE STEPS TO SUCCESS

Actually, you could help yourself by adopting any of the Power Principles and developing any of the Positive Addictions that I've listed below. You don't necessarily need to do them in any particular order. However, most of us have an easier time learning something one step at a time instead of all at once. So I've condensed all of the Power Principles and Positive Addictions into five easy steps. Each one of these steps helps you build attitudes and habits that are related to each other in particular ways and that will work together to give you mastery over certain kinds of situations. As we discuss each of these steps, I'll mention the Power Principles first and then the Positive Addictions that will empower you to put these principles into action.

Step 1: Do It with Attitude!

POWER PRINCIPLES

The Possibility Principle
I want to share with you a touching story of the innocence of children. This story involves a precious little girl—the daughter of one of my corporate motivation clients. This little girl is in third grade. She loves to sit on her father's lap when he reads aloud his motivational books. I'm proud to say he and his daughter often read my books and watch my videos together. That's what I call quality time! Despite all this wonderful family togetherness, the father never imagined that his little girl really understood what all those positive thinkers were saying.

Recently, he got the surprise of his life! His daughter returned from school with her latest exam in her hand. She had correctly answered nine out of ten questions. Naturally he was curious what she had gotten wrong.

What he found brought tears to his eyes—her error had been in defining the word "impossible." Her answer had been: "There is no such word. Nothing is impossible!"

That little girl had listened to me and my fellow motivators and, even at such a tender age, had absorbed our lessons well. She is the ultimate positive thinker—in the third grade! If only all my adult students were so willing to grasp the idea of the unlimited potential of the human race. You have much to learn from that precious little girl—you too must understand that nothing is impossible! Miracles happen every second of every day, all over the world. Now you must set your mind towards making your personal miracles come true! The next time you find yourself facing what seems like insurmountable odds, remember that:

> "Become a possibilitarian. No matter how dark things seem to be or actually are, raise our sights and see possibilities—always see them; for they're always there.
>
> *Norman Vincent Peale*

- A man with no legs walked the entire two-thousand-mile Appalachian Trail!

- A man paralyzed from the waist down rides horses in rodeo competitions!

- A female track star named Ana Quirot, burned badly over most of her body, told by doctors she'd never walk again—if she even lived—finished second in a major track event only months later. Two years later she won a gold medal at the World Championships.

A year after that she won a silver medal at the Olympics!

- Maria Serrao—who was paralyzed in an auto accident as a child—today models, acts (she has appeared on *General Hospital* and *21 Jump Street*), performs in beauty pageants (she was a pageant runner-up), hosts a cable television exercise show, has starred in two exercise videos, and is a national spokesperson for Cybex exercise equipment—all from her wheelchair.

- Cliff Meidel—who was jolted with thirty thousand volts of electricity and almost died three times, then almost had both badly burned legs amputated—marched in the opening ceremonies of the 1996 Summer Olympics—he made the U.S. Olympic Kayak Team!

- Bill Denby—who had both legs blown off in Vietnam—today plays in a basketball league on a team of handicapped athletes. He's even turned his handicap into an asset: He has starred in a national television advertising campaign.

- Jim Ward—who never ran a marathon in his life until age sixty-four—came in dead last in his age group in his first race. Thirteen years later he became the oldest person to finish "The Ironman Triathlon" in Hawaii!

- Dr. Jon Franks, my good friend, former chiropractor for numerous NBA teams—including the Lakers and

Celtics—was paralyzed from the waist down in a motorcycle accident. Despite losing the use of his lower body, Dr. Franks became the world's only wheelchair triathlete. That means he swims 2.4 miles, bikes 112 miles, and then finishes up by running a marathon—26.2 miles. He does all that without the benefit of his legs!

- Jerry Dunn, a recovering alcoholic, set an all-time record in 1996 by running twenty-six 26-mile marathons, 26 days in a row! He set another all-time record by running 104 marathons in one year!

- Shannon Lucid, who became the first American woman to live on the Russian Space Station Mir, set a United States space endurance record and became the first woman to fly in space five times! She accomplished all this at the age of fifty-three!

- Remember Arthur Hemingway, Jr., who was recruited by almost every major college football program in America in 1978. He chose to play fullback for the University of Southern California Trojans. But before he ever got to play a down of football, Art was hit by a felon speeding in a stolen car. He woke up from a month-long coma to find himself unable to walk. But eighteen years later—after twenty-two operations (including brain surgery twice) and bouts of obesity and depression—Art Hemingway, Jr. finally graduated from USC in 1996 with a 3.0 grade point average!

- Norm Johnson, at the age of ninety, lives in an apartment at the Pasadena Athletic Club and pumps iron every day! We've all heard that expression, "He practically lives at the gym!" But here's a ninety year old who literally *does* live at the gym! He's a man after my own heart—and I'm proud to say he's my adopted grandfather!

- Kathy Hogencamp, who fought numerous handicaps to win election to the Kentucky State Assembly, was elected to an all-Democratic district despite being a woman, a Republican, and disabled! She is not only the first Republican elected in her district since the Civil War, but the first person in a wheelchair elected to the State House in a quarter-century.

- Manny Wein ran in his fifth L.A. Marathon one month before his ninetieth birthday.

- Former three-time world motorcycle racing champion Wayne Rainey, despite being paralyzed from the waist down, now owns his own racing team and raced a Toyota Celica GT in the Long Beach Celebrity Grand Prix.

- John Lucas, who only a decade ago was waived twice from the NBA for drug use and had drifted in and out of four drug treatment centers, is today celebrating his tenth year of sobriety as head coach of the Philadelphia 76ers!

- Tyronee (Tiger) Bussey, Jr., who was diagnosed in 1994 with leukemia, had a ruptured appendix, deteriorated colon, and a collapsed immune system. He underwent a bone marrow transplant, got sick with double pneumonia, and finally he fell into a coma—and less than a year later he was back in uniform tackling runners and sacking quarterbacks for the Colorado Buffaloes!

These examples prove that anything is possible. They prove there are no limits. They prove that no one can stop you from attaining your goals or achieving your dreams. They prove that your past doesn't affect your future. They prove that anything you can conceive, you can achieve. Each of these individuals are THRIVERS. They all faced insurmountable odds. They all overcame daunting disabilities. Yet they found a way to change the world—to THRIVE. So what are you waiting for?

> "Some men see things as they are and say, 'Why?' I dream of things that never were and say, 'Why not?'"
>
> *George Bernard Shaw*

Start dreaming big, planning big, risking big, failing big, and achieving big! Anything is possible.

The Positive Principle

Turning the impossible into the possible is all about attitude—positive attitude! Is the glass half full or half empty? Of course, it's half full! That's positive attitude! That's how you create the impossible. That's how you overcome immovable obstacles! Life is all about attitude—how you choose to see things. Let me give you a few examples.

Did you know that legal immigrants in the United States are four times more likely to become millionaires than those of us lucky enough to be born in America? Isn't that shocking? What do you make of that eye-opening, illusion-shattering statistic? The answer is actually quite simple: It's all about attitude! Legal immigrants have overcome great hardship to get to America. They have often risked starvation, death, and loss of their families. America was their dream. They intently focused on that dream for decades. Once they've turned that dream into reality, they refuse to be stopped or denied. Where others see prejudice and problems, immigrants see only opportunity. They have tunnel vision—they were told for years that America was the land of opportunity. They want to believe so desperately that they create opportunity where there is none! While those born here have been told again and again that the American dream is dead and start to believe it, legal immigrants have been told over and over again that America's streets are paved with gold—and they believe it! It is nothing more than this attitude that empowers them to achieve. With the right attitude you can change the way you look, you can change your life, you can even change the world! Nothing is impossible— as long as you believe in your power to make it happen!

For those of you who still have doubts, I must present a story that still today brings a smile to my face. It was back in 1983 that I first met Doug Miller. I've told you about Doug—he was and still is the biggest influence in my life. At the time we first met I was young, impressionable, and broke—I was in the midst of failing and flailing. I was invited to a real estate meeting at Doug's home and I fell in love with his lifestyle. There was Doug living the life of my dreams. He was doing business in his silk robe, with a cordless phone in each hand—outside in the sunshine of his backyard. His wife and newborn son Alexander (my godson) were playing a few feet away. I thought I'd died and gone to heaven—this was the life for me! I kept that image in my mind for the next decade. Every time I struggled or faced more disappointment, I visualized that image to get me back on track. I knew what my goal was and I knew I had to stay committed. I visualized my own version of that "perfect" lifestyle a few thousand times during my painful journey. It is what kept me going. Today, I have turned my dreams into a reality. I went out and replicated that image. I turned that dream into my reality.

> **"The great things in life are not achieved with what is in our head. They are achieved with what is in our heart, our spirit, our will."**
>
> *Wayne Allyn Root*

There was one small problem with that image, however—it was totally, completely false! You see, years later when I thanked Doug for serving as my role model, he laughed and told me that at the time we met, he was going through the worst period of his life. He was out of work and desperately pursuing new career opportunities. He was working out of his home for only one reason: He had no other choice! He actually couldn't wait to get out of his house and back to a real office. He was going stir-crazy. Doug was my role model—I believed that if he did it, so could I. If I had known the truth, I might never have succeeded. I turned my dream into reality because I believed— I had faith! That's the power of a positive attitude. That's the power of faith. That's the power of a dream. It doesn't even matter if your dream is based on reality—as long as you believe with all your heart and soul! My entire dream was based on an illusion. But yours is not. I am living proof that anyone can combine family, faith, and a home office. Now it's your turn!

> **"The greatest discovery of my generation is that a human being can alter his life by altering his attitude."**
> *Hannibal*

The Lemonade Principle
This principle is all about turning lemons into lemonade. The Lemonade Principle is also an attitude—it is the attitude of a THRIVER. The word *no* is not an immovable obstacle to a THRIVER. It is simply an invitation to turn failure and rejection into extraordinary success. Everyone fails—it is the ability to overcome failure that separates THRIVERS (or successful failures) from the rest of us! Let me give you some examples:

Fran and John Burt are masters of the Lemonade Principle. A forty-ton boulder careened down a hill last year in a small town called Fountain City, Wisconsin. The rock smashed into a home, wiping out the master bedroom. The couple inside ran for their lives. They returned only to pack—selling the house at a drastic price reduction. The buyers—Fran and John Burt—saw opportunity where others saw disaster. They turned their new home into a tourist attraction—over twelve thousand visitors paid one dollar each to view "The Rock in the House"! That's twelve thousand dollars profit—six times the two thousand dollar cost of removing the rock! If all goes well, the Burts can remove the rock, renovate the bedroom, and resell

> **"The successful man will profit from his mistakes and try again in a different way."**
>
> *Dale Carnegie*

the house at a price far above what they paid—and still have several thousand dollars left over. Now that's turning big rocks into big bucks.

Gina Rugolo of More MeDavoy Management is a Hollywood talent manager. Her story is about turning lemons into lemonade—Hollywood style! She had the bad luck of representing five actresses—all pregnant at the same time. Now any normal Hollywood talent manager would have cursed fate and accepted the idea of earning no income for the next year, but not Rugolo. Instead of losing tens of thousands of dollars in commissions, she came up with the unique idea of packaging all five actresses into a movie about pregnancy! She also found a pregnant female producer to produce the movie! Then she went out and pitched the movie to potential sponsors—who else but baby food companies? Now that's turning growing bellies into growing bank accounts!

Then there's the example of a company called Upper Limits in Bloomington, Illinois. Farmers are a dying breed—experts predict America will lose more farm jobs in the next decade than any other occupation. That's bad news for areas of the country dependent on farming—particularly the Midwest. There are abandoned grain silos all over the farm belt. But Upper Limits found a way to turn a negative into a positive. They bought fourteen abandoned silos—worthless eyesores filled with rotting grain. They then removed six tons of rotten grain and twelve tons of steel. Finally they converted the former silos into indoor climbing facilities in the summer and ice climbing facilities in the winter (after watering them down). Now they get several hundred climbers a week (remember, the Midwest is flat—there's nowhere else to climb), paying them ten dollars each! That's turning rotten grain into a cash crop!

You've all heard of the hit movie *Back to the Future*—how about a success story called "Back to the Profits"! Virginia Rogers suffered from debilitating back pain her whole life. Then she found a small store in Austin, Texas, specializing in back pain relief items. She bought products that eased her pain—until she found out the store was going broke. Then she got a headache too! But she solved both problems by buying the bankrupt store for fifteen thousand dollars. By last year she had sold over forty-five franchises and generated $15 million in annual revenues! That's turning debilitating pain into exhilarating gain!

Then there's talk show hostess Kathie Lee Gifford, who was attacked in the press by human rights activists for putting her name on a clothing line produced by young children paid low wages in sweatshops. But instead of denying the problem or running away from negative publicity, Kathie Lee turned the controversy into her very own passionate cause. She is now in the forefront of the movement to expose, condemn, and correct human rights violations in the garment industry. She has joined Labor Secretary Robert Reich to lobby Congress to shut down sweatshops and ban products produced by underage children. That's turning human suffering into human compassion!

But no story of lemons turned to lemonade is more touching or heartbreaking than that of baseball Hall of Famer Rod Carew and his beautiful daughter, Michelle. Michelle died at the young age of eighteen of a rare form of leukemia. But before she died, Michelle made a wonderful mark on the world. She will forever be remembered as a hero. Michelle's plight and her father's poignant pleas for help attracted news media headlines throughout the world. The desperate search for a bone marrow donor failed Michelle. But that same search sparked worldwide donor interest. The National Marrow Donor Program received over seventy thousand calls within days of Michelle's diagnosis. In just the first few hours after her tragic death, nearly three thousand potential donors came forward! Brave Michelle Carew and her loving father turned a tragic death into the gift of life!

When I look back on my career, I see the same principles at work again and again. A missed opportunity at NBC Radio turned into a book deal and television career. A missed opportunity at Fox TV turned into my national television debut on FNN Sports. And a lifetime of pain, rejection, and failure turned into a book called *The Joy of Failure!* If I didn't turn lemons into lemonade, you wouldn't be sitting here reading my book! Because of all the failures I faced, many others will enjoy success!

> "Every problem has in it the seeds of its own solution. If you don't have any problems, you don't get any seeds."
>
> *Norman Vincent Peale*

Finally, I'll use my beautiful wife Debra as the ultimate example of turning lemons into lemonade. Debra is a knockout—blonde, beautiful, bright. She speaks five languages fluently. She is a gourmet cook. A great mother. And to top it off, a former Miss Oklahoma! But life wasn't always ideal for my wife. She suffered from weight problems for almost her entire youth. As a young child, she was overweight. As a teenager, she yo-yoed between overweight and underweight. She suffered from both anorexia and bulimia. By her twenties, she had recovered from all her problems and turned into a beautiful young woman. But she was not out of the woods yet. Soon after marrying me, she found herself in the middle of a stress whirlwind. Debra had never been around an Energizer Bunny before! She'd never been asked to do twelve things at once—while the phone rang a hundred times a day and the fax machine spit out letters from dawn to dusk. Add the death of both of my parents, the open-heart surgery of her father, the birth of our daughter, and the Los Angeles riots all in a one-month period! My wife was overwhelmed. (Can you blame her?) Her reaction was to revert back to her childhood. She ate to deal with the pressures she was facing and gained eighty pounds during the pregnancy. For over two years after giving birth she could not lose the weight—despite starvation diets, a torturous exercise schedule, and expensive personal trainers. Nothing worked. Then she realized that losing weight wasn't about obsession. She had to change her lifestyle and attitude—she had to deal with the stress and emotions that caused her to eat when she wasn't truly hungry. She had to literally become a new person—she'd have to relearn how to live. So she started praying, meditating, affirming, visualizing, eating a healthy, low-fat diet (without starving or obsessing), and moderately exercising! She started living my program. The pounds started to melt off!

Before long, Debra was back to being Debra again. But she did more than lose weight—she also turned her experiences into a company called Mrs. Malibu, Inc.! Today that company sells books, cookbooks, non-fat foods, and most importantly, a nonfat peanut butter which Debra invented herself! Debra's products will be available in supermarkets nationwide by late 1996! That's turning a lifelong weight problem into a heavy-weight solution!

Life comes down to failure and rejection. Those who wallow in their pain, who complain or who give up, are destined to live disappointing lives. Those who take action and find creative solutions to their disappointments and challenges are THRIVERS. And their reward is the life of their dreams! That's the life I recommend you choose to live!

The Self-Esteem Principle

Self-esteem is all about confidence—feeling good about yourself and believing in your ability to make your dreams come true. Your level of self-confidence determines the way others see you. The way you choose to see yourself, virtually without exception, is also the image you will project to others. If *you* don't believe in you, why would anyone else? If *you* don't love you, why should anyone else? If *you* don't think of yourself as a winner, who would pick you to join their team? To head their project? To share their life? Your self-image will affect your goals, your career, your relationships, your entire life! Let's be honest—extraordinary success just doesn't go hand in hand with depression, negativity, self-loathing, and self-destructive behavior! That's why positive self-esteem—

"Don't find a fault. Find a remedy."

Henry Ford

confidence—is at the core of my philosophy. Without it, you can't attract others. Without it, you'll never have staying power. If deep down inside you are insecure, you'll pack up your tent at the first sign of rejection. All your worst fears will come true again and again. If deep down inside you hate yourself—you're self-destructive—you'll find a way to ruin your success and happiness every time something good comes your way! If your goal is success—THRIVING—you must think of yourself as a success. You must expect success. You must feel deep down inside that you deserve success. You must live, eat, breathe, and smell success twenty-four hours a day!

The Appreciation Principle

The key to feeling good about yourself is forcing yourself to find the blessings in your life. To be successful, you need to be positive and confident. You will need to spread the good word—brag about the blessings in your life to others. You will need to share good news to lighten the load of others and brighten their day. To be confident, you must find reasons to be happy. You must go out of your way to appreciate the things in your life that are positive. You must always see the glass as half full—no matter how gloomy things seem, there's always something to be thankful for. If instead you stress the negative, you'll spend your life on Prozac, Lithium, and Valium.

The Optimism Principle

This principle is a corollary to the Appreciation Principle. While appreciation is all about seeing the blessings and positives in your life, the Optimism Principle is all about seeing the positives in the world around you. I believe the reason many of us are so depressed and cynical is that we are bombarded daily by the news media with stories and images that depict the worst of society. Yes, there are gangbangers, rapists, murderers, carjackers, welfare moms, homeless people, and ruthless drug cartels—not only do they exist, there are more of them than ever before. But they are still a minuscule portion of our world—good people who obey the law and raise healthy families still outnumber the dysfunctional outcasts by 1,000 to 1. But you wouldn't know it by watching talk shows, soap operas, and the evening news. There is good all around us—heartwarming stories that reaffirm life, love, beauty, and God. But you rarely, if ever, see those stories on television. As we all spend more and more of our precious time in front of the boob tube, our subconscious minds are bombarded with images of fear, death, destruction, and moral decay. Deep down—even if we have faith and confidence in ourselves—we start to distrust, dislike, and feel depressed about our world. That fear and loathing starts to affect our attitude. Optimism fades. Our hope for our children's future erodes. We feel lousy all day, every day. That feeling of despair permeates our lives—everything we do is tinged with that sour feeling.

> **"I am an optimist. It does not seem too much use being anything else."**
> *Winston Churchill*

I want you to feel good again. To feel hope again. I want you to realize there's a whole other side of the picture you've never been exposed to. The good news far outweighs the bad. We live in a great world! We are blessed to be alive in a phenomenal time and place. Being alive today is one of the great opportunities in the history of mankind. In fact, the opportunities that lay before you and me are limitless. The good news far outweighs the bad. Here's a dose of good news that the news media, naysayers, and the "doom and gloomers" have no interest in sharing with you:

Yes, there is poverty among us. But there always has been. The "poor" that politicians, the news media, and human rights activists scream and cry about all day long (remember, the more they can depress and alarm you, the more security they have for their jobs or positions of authority) have never—in the history of civilization—been better off! Ninety-three percent of those classified as "poor" in America have color televisions. (That's the good news. The bad news is they spend too much time watching them.) Seventy-two percent own washing machines. Sixty percent own air conditioners. Sixty-four percent own a car. Forty percent of "the poor" own their own homes. Yes, we'd all like to eradicate poverty. But never before have people with so many modern comforts and conveniences been classified as "poor." And being poor is far from a death sentence. A new study tracking fifty thousand Americans who in 1975 were mired in poverty found that by 1991 only 5 percent were still living in poverty! Not only did a majority of the poor join the middle class, almost 30 percent had joined the top level of income earners!

Yes, there is a health care crisis. Yet never before have doctors, hospitals, and medical professionals had more advanced tools at their disposal. Never before have so many individuals had access to the best of modern science. Never before have you and I—in the history of civilization—had the opportunity to live this long.

So why are we all so fearful? So depressed? We should be jumping for joy and thanking God that we are alive in an age of so many blessings and so much promise. No one gives us reasons to celebrate—so we don't.

Yes, there is racism and discrimination. No, we shouldn't rest until it's wiped off the face of the earth. But did you know that the number of African-American home buyers qualifying for mortgages jumped almost 60 percent between 1993 and 1996? That's a fact that didn't manage to lead off your evening news report.

Yes, there is discrimination towards women. But did you know that despite all the prejudice and challenges women face in the business world, one out of every four workers in America is employed by a female business owner? Did you know women own one third of all businesses in America? That sales for female-owned businesses are up 236 percent since 1987? That's 2.28 *trillion* dollars! Why aren't these facts trumpeted by the politicians and news media? Because if they didn't paralyze you with fear, they're afraid you wouldn't read their paper, watch their network, or vote for them anymore! They have to keep you paralyzed with fear to keep their jobs!

Yes, life is more competitive than ever before—that's a fact! But look at the payoff: There are more Americans taking vacations than ever before. The number of American workers receiving paid vacations is the highest it's ever been. Twice as many of us are retired from work. Twice as many own boats. Eight times as many own recreational vehicles (RVs). There are more golfers than ever before. There are more people taking cruises than ever before. More of us are flying on airplanes than ever before. We have more amazing, modern conveniences than anyone could have imagined only five or ten years ago. How did anyone survive? Thank God we have them today! Yet we're depressed, angry, and bitter?

We are blessed—for the first time in the history of mankind—with the freedom to work from anywhere in the world. With personal computers, faxes, pagers, cellular phones, laptops, e-mail, and the Internet, I can earn a living in my "virtual office" overlooking the beach in Malibu or on a mountaintop in Aspen! I want to shout with joy from the highest mountain: I am blessed! So are you. The opportunities that lie before you and me are limitless. Yet you're depressed and unhappy? Why? You take these blessings for granted. Why?

Think about it for a minute or two. Why are you unhappy? What's so bad about living in our world today? Start thinking up reasons to be optimistic instead of pessimistic. Look for the good in others, in your life, in the world around you. Then sit back and watch the miracles unfold before your eyes—your new and improved attitude will attract blessings and opportunities you never thought possible. Stop looking for the worst—I guarantee that if you're looking for the worst, you'll find it. Start looking for the best—pretty soon it'll fill your life!

The Think Big Principle

I've gone to great lengths in this book to drum home the point that failure can be positive. I have presented dozens of examples of individuals who went on to great success after experiencing devastating failure. But what else besides failure did all these successful failures have in common? What set them apart from ordinary failures? The answer is that they all lived by the Think Big Principle! Think about it. When Abraham Lincoln and Winston Churchill failed again and again, they were still in a position to succeed big. Why? They were playing in the big leagues. If your goal is to become president or prime minister, you can afford a few failures along the way. There is room for a margin of error. And if you never achieve your goal, you have a high expectation of winding up as congressperson, senator, governor, or a cabinet head.

Frank Sinatra and George Burns may have endured a lot of failure, but look at the payoff they faced when they finally succeeded. When your goal is national television star or matinee idol and you succeed, the payoff is a lifetime of fame and fortune. Sly Stallone may have been a starving actor and screenwriter early in his career, but at least he was playing for high stakes. When he finally succeeded, he succeeded big! Greg Norman—the golfing legend known as "The Shark"— has actually set records for failure and futility. His collapses in the late rounds of major tournaments are legendary. His spectacular collapse in the final round of the 1996 Masters may go down as the worst ever. But in the end, it is Norman who has the last laugh. All that collapsing has still lead to a dream life—millions in golf winnings, tens of millions in endorsements, millions in clothing sales. Failure isn't so bad, when it happens at the top! At the highest levels of competition, losing still makes you a millionaire. But the key is that you've got to aim high and find a way to get to those highest levels!

When I look around at many of my students and clients, I see a common mistake: they aim too low. Whether it's due to fear (which forces them to settle for a mediocre job), low self-esteem, or simply lack of support (no one ever told them to aim high and think big), I often see individuals who lack confidence and drive. They are playing at levels on which they'll never see any big results. If you're aiming for the curb and you miss, you'll be left in the gutter. Even if you succeed, what have you accomplished? Who wants to spend life at curb-level? But if you aim for the stars—if you strive to be the best at whatever you do—and you miss, you'll still land on the moon! And if you hit, you've got the life of your dreams! The point of all this is rather simple— the higher you aim in life, the better the chance you'll land safely, even after a failure or rejection. People who aim high are THRIVERS!

THRIVERS all think big! So big, it's often hard to imagine! Let me give you a few examples—I'm proud to say all of the following individuals are close friends of mine. THRIVERS attract other THRIVERS like a magnet!

Dr. Jay Gordon has turned thinking big into an art form! Jay is my daughter Dakota's pediatrician—a children's doctor. That in and of itself is impressive. But Jay wouldn't settle for just being a doctor. He spent five years as medical expert for ABC's *Home Show*. When that show ended, he could have gone back to his practice and quietly practiced his craft. But Jay kept hustling. He wound up as medical expert on *Home & Family* on the Family Channel. He starred in his own television infomercial called, "Good Food Today, Great Kids Tomorrow." And in the fall of 1996 his own line of vitamins called "Pediatricians' Choice" will be released nationwide! This guy isn't a doctor, he's a conglomerate!

Dr. Don Altfeld is another big-thinking friend of mine. Also a doctor—I'm no dummy, I choose my friends wisely!—he's also a human dynamo. There are tens of thousands of doctors in America—99.99 percent are satisfied practicing medicine. Not my friends! Don happened to write "Little Old Lady From Pasadena" for the Beach Boys while going to medical school! It became a number one hit for Jan & Dean! Don still rakes in royalties to this day. But that wasn't enough for him either. You see, Dr. Don has had a lifetime love affair with rock 'n' roll music and the People's Republic of China. He found a way to combine the two: he is now CEO of China USA. His company is the exclusive distributor of American country and rock 'n' roll music on China National Radio! China USA just signed a deal with Disney to market all of Disney's products on a new radio show in China! It will be called, "It's a Small World!" When was the last time you met a doctor who in his spare time wrote hit songs and introduced the Beatles, Garth Brooks, Mickey Mouse and Donald Duck to a billion Chinese?

Phil Strenkowski is another of my good friends who thinks big. Phil was a cop—a Los Angeles County sheriff's deputy. There are hundreds of thousands of police officers in America. Most have never met a celebrity in their lives. Many retire and live off a meager pension for the rest of their lives. Not Phil. He made sure he was a police officer assigned to Malibu, California. Soon he was setting up charity events like "Code Three for Kids"—pitting police officers against the biggest celebrities in Hollywood to raise money for homeless kids. Phil recruited these celebs right from the streets of Malibu! He met them when he pulled them over for speeding or when he'd handle a disturbance or break-in at their houses. Phil never missed an opportunity to network. Instead of being "just a cop," Phil promoted himself into the title of "Police Officer to the Stars!" Phil, a black belt in karate, also invented a personal safety device called The Key. It fits on a key chain and empowers women to protect themselves in case of assault. Today, Phil leads the retirement of his dreams—he travels the world providing security for the celebrities and rock stars he met while patrolling the streets of Malibu—except now he's paid several thousands of dollars a week! And he sells his safety product, "The Key" in stores across the country! Phil thinks big!

Finally, I'd like to mention the story of one of my wife's best friends, Dena Weiss. Dena is an attorney. But the story of how she became an attorney is nothing short of remarkable. Dena was nine months pregnant when she took her bar exam! But when you think big, nothing is impossible. She informed the state of California of her situation and her rights as a mother-to-be, and she was allowed to take the bar in a bed wheeled into a special bar exam room—with a doctor standing by. While half of all lawyers need two or three tries to pass the bar (JFK Jr., for one), Dena passed on her first try—under the most trying of circumstances! She actually went into the first stages of labor during the last day of testing. Only a few years later she went on to represent a group of plaintiffs in a famous police brutality case that resulted in a record-shattering multimillion dollar judgment! Most lawyers will never see a settlement like that in a lifetime of practice. Dena did it in her first decade of practice!

I learned to think big at a very young age. Almost from the day I was old enough to walk, my father taught me and my sister to aim high—to expect the best. We were literally programmed on a daily basis to believe we would attend an Ivy League college—Columbia University, to be specific. And darned if my father the butcher didn't send not one, but remarkably two children to Columbia University! In all of America, I'd guess there isn't another butcher who raised two Ivy League graduates! My sister is today a successful attorney. She also graduated Columbia Law School!

The Pimple Principle
One of the keys to patience is the understanding that no one is perfect. Many of us get bogged down in the

process by spending too much time and wasting too much energy focusing on our limitations and weaknesses—our pimples. We all have talents and by the same token, we all have flaws. We are all incompetent at some things. My advice is to find the things you're good at and the things you're not. Then immerse yourself in the ones that make you shine. Avoid the others like the plague!

Since you are now reading my book, I've got to assume you think I'm talented and insightful. You must want to share my insights. You must think my philosophy and strategies can empower your life! Yet I'm totally incompetent at so many different things:

- I can't type.

- I'm far from a computer whiz. I can barely find my way on the Internet.

- I'm lousy at math. I don't even remember algebra, geometry, or trig. Thank God for calculators.

- I stink at *Jeopardy*. I feel like a real dummy most of the time—especially when my wife gets all of the answers!

- I have no mechanical ability whatsoever. I can't change the oil in my car. I can't perform simple household repairs. I leave all repairs for my wife!

- I cannot—for the life of me—read a map. I have no sense of direction.

- I can't read music.

- Up until a few years ago, I could not swim.

- My passion for golf is not matched by my talent for playing golf.

- I'm a terrible cook—thank God my wife is a gourmet cook. If not, I'm sure my daughter and I would starve to death!

- I'm horrible at learning languages—I have enough trouble with basic English!

- I stink at basketball. I can't dribble and run at the same time.

- I am an awful singer. My voice makes dogs cover their ears with their paws.

- As a baseball player, I was a sensational fielder, but I couldn't hit worth a darn.

The list of my flaws, or "pimples," is twice as long as my attributes. Yet the few things I'm good at—namely motivating and communicating—gave me the life of my dreams!

The same holds true for other successful super-achievers. I doubt Whitney Houston has changed the oil in her limo lately. I doubt Bill Gates will ever win a Grammy for his singing. I haven't heard Madonna speaking Chinese lately. Donald Trump won't make the U.S. Olympic team. Joe Montana isn't going to set any records on *Jeopardy*. Pavarotti is a world-class singer, but I wonder how proficient he is on the Internet? Bill Clinton probably doesn't do windows.

So don't get down on yourself for the things you can't do well. Learn to appreciate the things you're talented at. All you need is one talent. Build your life around that talent. Ignore the rest! You'll have higher self-esteem. You'll have a little more patience. Your attitude will be more positive. You'll smile a lot more. You'll treat the people you love with more respect. You'll sleep a lot better at night!

The Preparation Principle

Life often comes down to a few precious moments of opportunity. Are you ready? Are you prepared? When that one moment presents itself, will you come up big?

There are no overnight successes. That's one of the big myths of our society. It takes decades of practice and preparation to achieve overnight success. When you watch a concert pianist, is it God-given natural talent you are viewing or two decades of practice? The latter, of course. When you watch the Olympics and you see a graceful ice-skater, is it God-given talent or thousands of hours of routines on a cold ice rink at 6 A.M.? The latter, of course. When you go on your annual ski vacation and someone goes skiing by at the speed of light, is it God-given natural talent or is it thousands of hours of practice on ski slopes—perhaps in concert with a professional ski instructor? The latter, of course.

Talent helps. So does God. But mostly, God just helps those who help themselves: The more you practice, the more help you happen to get from God!

Don't get depressed or discouraged because you're not as good as that pianist, ice-skater, or skier. There's something in this world you were born to do. Find it and then give it everything you've got. Be prepared, so that on the day opportunity presents itself, you'll be in a position to capitalize big-time. And that goes doubly for relationships—don't sit around and bemoan your lack of options. Spend your time preparing for that one moment of opportunity. Taking action and searching out Mr. or Ms. Right is one thing—but when you find him or her, will he or she like you? What do you offer them? Are you educated enough? Are you attractive enough? Fashionable enough? Is your energy and passion high enough? Your job is to spend your life preparing for important moments of opportunity. At that moment, be sure you are the best you can possibly be! Be sure you are the definition of a THRIVER!

POSITIVE ADDICTIONS

Be a Prayer Addict!

I've said it before. I'll say it again. Prayer is the foundation of my life. Without it, I'd be lost. I've already explained why I believe prayer to be so powerful and effective. Now I'd like to share my input on how to utilize prayer more effectively and efficiently.

First and foremost, do it! As part of your new disciplined lifestyle, schedule a specific time to pray every morning and every night. I pray every morning within minutes of awakening. I know that if I don't schedule it and do it—first thing in the morning and last thing at night—it won't get done. The phone will ring, my daughter will need my help, my wife will need me to run an errand, a business associate will schedule a meeting with me—there's always something. And I'll lose that window of opportunity for prayer.

> **"Work as if you will live a hundred years. Pray as if you would die tomorrow."**
>
> *Benjamin Franklin*

I need that foundation before beginning a long, stressful day of work. Without it, I'm lost, I'm angry, I'm quick-tempered, I'm stressed out. With prayer, I'm a different person—more loving, more compassionate, more focused, less apt to snap at others. Prayer is so important to my mental well-being, I cannot skip it. So I schedule it and I do it—period!

Another way to effectively utilize prayer is to schedule it throughout the day to alleviate stress. Praying at the start of the day may reduce stress, but you'll need to pray more often during times of intense pressure. When I receive bad news, get into heated discussions, or face stressful deadlines (like when I was writing this book), I pray several times throughout the day—even if only for a few seconds or minutes. Prayer is a miracle for me. It instantly changes my attitude and lifts my spirits. It instantly lifts the burden off my shoulders. The moment I pray, I feel a subtle change in my psyche.

Begin to utilize prayer to sustain you in difficult or fearful moments or times of stress. Use it any time you

or need. It's free and you don't have to ask
permission!

, my experiences with prayer have led me to
a powerful new twist. I've separated prayer
o distinct categories: spontaneous and ordered.
"Spontaneous prayer" is when I simply talk to God off
the cuff. I take a morning walk in the mountains or a
sunset stroll on the beach. I'm the only one there and I
pray out loud about the thoughts, wishes, and worries
on my mind. It's like having the world's greatest lis-
tener on your side. Who needs psychiatrists? I lay all
the troubles I'm feeling or experiencing at that moment
on God. Magically, my conscience is
cleared and my stress is alleviated.

> **"God is everywhere
> and in everything
> and without Him we
> cannot exist."**
>
> *Mother Teresa*

"Ordered prayer" is a new wrinkle
I've created that has made a tremendous difference in my life. Ordered
simply means that I design a set
prayer—personalized just for me and
my wishes. I set aside an hour every three months and
I sit someplace quiet and inspirational—overlooking
the ocean, in the woods, at the beach, etc.—to write an
ordered prayer that feels right to me. A prayer that
talks to my soul and my needs, at this particular time
and place in my life. Usually it's three to five pages
long. Then I set aside the time to read it aloud for five
to ten minutes every morning upon awakening. That
way, it's simple. I wrote it in an enlightened state and
it's there for me to repeat again and again, every single
morning. No deep thought required, nothing important

left out. My words of wisdom, my goals, my wishes, my worries, set down in writing to repeat again and again.

Every three months I update and/or revise my ordered prayers. That way my morning dialogue is fresh and applicable to my personal agenda at that moment in time. Believe me when I tell you that ordered prayer makes praying simpler and more effective. You schedule it every day at the same time(s), the prayer is there written out for you, it addresses your unique problems, and you do it. The next step is the best one of all—your newfound faith changes your attitude and your life!

Now that you've decided to become a prayer addict, take a few moments to answer the following questions.

- How do I feel about God and prayer?

- Have I properly utilized prayer in the past, when facing stress and challenge?

- If not, why not?

- What difference has faith made in my life?

- What difference could a renewed emphasis on faith make in the future?

- What could I do to best utilize prayer in my life from this day forward?

- If I were to start each day with prayer, what impact would that have on my life?

- What impact might it have on others?

- Do I see a connection between a faith in God and a healthier, happier future?

- Do I see the connection between a faith in God and a more positive outlook on life?

- What might that positive outlook on life do for my future?

- Where will I design my ordered prayer?

- What are the issues, problems, and wishes I'd like to start discussing daily with God?

- Will scheduling prayer as a Positive Addiction make it more effective for me? How?

- At what time(s) will I schedule prayer each day?

- What is the connection between faith and prayer and achieving more financial success?

- Would a better relationship with God affect my business performance?

- How would this new relationship affect my dealings with clients, customers, or fellow workers?

- How will it affect my ability to communicate ideas to others?

- Will it enhance my ability to sell my skills or my product to others?

- Will it enhance my leadership skills?

• How will it affect the way others view me?

• Will prayer affect how I view myself?

Be a Meditation Addict!

If you're interested in a powerful one-two punch, it doesn't get more powerful than prayer combined with meditation. I perform both of these addictions each morning when I arise. They are so important to my mental health and well-being, they are the first two things I do after I open my eyes!

> "All that happens in world history rests on something spiritual. If the spiritual is strong, it creates world history. If it is weak, it suffers world history."
>
> *Albert Schweitzer*

The benefits of meditation mirror the benefits of prayer. Like prayer, meditation helps you to be both calmer and clearer. Like prayer, meditation empowers you to be more creative and focused. Like prayer, meditation relieves stress and, in doing so, creates a more positive outlook on life. Like prayer, the positive state of mind you create through meditation keeps you healthier—mentally, physically, and spiritually. Like prayer, meditation allows you to go deep inside yourself and tap into amazing ideas, wisdom, and understanding you never knew you had. Like prayer, once you quiet down and look inward, you'll find strength and wisdom that will empower you.

So what exactly is meditation? Why do I tie it so closely to prayer? I believe meditation is just another form of prayer. When you pray, you go to a quiet place and talk to God. That dialogue with God calms you and gives you strength and confidence. When you meditate you also get quiet. By thinking of nothing and concentrating only on your breathing, you quiet your mind down. Suddenly it is free to tap into your innate wisdom and the messages you're receiving from God. That's right, I believe all of us receive messages from God all the time! There's an ongoing dialogue between you and your maker—you just have to get quiet enough, focused enough, and centered enough to hear it! So in that way, both prayer and meditation accomplish the same thing—establishing a deep inner dialogue between you and God's wisdom.

> **"Looking for the fountain of youth? Consider meditation."**
>
> *USA Today*

Is meditation complicated or difficult? Once again, I've taken something regarded by some as mysterious and complicated (like prayer, discipline, and goal planning) and made it simple. Most of us do not have thirty to sixty minutes to meditate. The good news is you don't need that much time. You can get the benefits of meditation from just a few minutes a day! And you can refresh and reenergize your spirits with short two to three minute mini-meditations throughout the day. You can meditate anywhere—at home, in your office, in the pool or Jacuzzi, in the bathtub or your bed—and like prayer it doesn't cost a dime! As long as you can find a place to sit quietly and breathe, you can meditate!

How do you do it? It's easy. Let me show you how I do it:

First you find a quiet place or room in your house. I recommend doing it early in the morning, before your children or spouse wake up, or during the day, when the kids are at school. You can even do it at your office, if you can close the door and ask for no interruptions for ten or fifteen minutes. Next put on a tape, record, or CD of music that soothes, relaxes, and inspires. Set a timer or alarm clock for ten to fifteen minutes for your main daily meditation. I'd recommend starting at ten and building up to fifteen minutes.

Now sit up straight in your chair or lie down flat on your back. Keep a straight vertical line with your head and spine. Now start by saying a short prayer. Ask God for help in calming and focusing yourself. Ask for the concentration to go deep within. Ask for the ability to hear the wisdom and messages coming from God. Ask for quiet and no interruptions. Ask for strength. This is the transition you will need to make the difficult jump from a stressful day to a place of mental calmness.

Next, close your eyes. Become aware of your body. Begin to breathe in deeply and slowly. Feel your breath. Concentrate on each breath. You might want to count to eight on the inhale, hold for eight beats, then count to eight on the exhale. Or you might be more comfortable focusing on an unspoken word or sound with each breath: amen, God, love, safe, peace, or any word that makes you feel positive. Repeat the word slowly on each breath in and each breath out. That's it. That is how you meditate! It's not complicated or mysterious. Simply do it until the timer or clock rings. You

> **"...in quietness and confidence shall be your strength."**
> *Isaiah 30:15*

will feel refreshed, energized, motivated, positive, and focused. The positive feelings you experience will get stronger each time you meditate. And the results will last longer each time too. It's just like playing sports—the more you practice it, the better you'll get at it and the more you'll get out of it.

What does meditation do? It simply stops the negative chatter going on in your subconscious mind all day long. Your mind is busy—a nonstop talking machine. Meditation blocks out those thoughts. It distracts and quiets your mind. Studies have proven that a few minutes of meditation are equal to a few hours of quality sleep. Your mind is tired and overused. It needs the rest. A lifetime of meditation will take years of wear and tear off your mind. You'll reduce stress and anxiety. You'll look better and feel better. You'll get sick less often—stress causes most sickness and disease. You'll add years to your life span. Nothing we can do to improve our lives is more important than finding a positive and healthy way to deal with stress. Meditation is that way.

There is a complication to all this, though. Sitting still for even ten minutes is not as easy as it sounds. You may start tapping your feet, twitching your legs, or itching. Your mind will definitely wander—it's never been quieted or controlled before. It will rebel and try to gain back control from you. It doesn't want to be quiet—it wants to chatter endlessly and incessantly. That's what it's done since you were born; now it wants its freedom back. It will try to win the battle of wills by distracting you; your mind will wander into thoughts about your business, relationships, bills, children, etc. Your mind is smart; it knows how to get your attention.

Don't get angry or frustrated. Simply ignore the thoughts and go back to concentrating on your breathing. After a few seconds, the thoughts will disappear. In a few minutes the chatter and distractions will start all over again. Simply ignore the distractions and breathe deep again. Let them float gently away. The more you meditate, the easier it will be to eliminate the interruptions. Your subconscious mind will eventually put aside the noisy, negative, stressful chatter. After a while your mind will come to enjoy the quiet—it will crave the time off! That's when you'll start to access your most positive, loving, insightful, and creative thoughts.

> **"Employees from the executive suite to the factory floor are using meditation to calm their minds and relieve the health-threatening effects of job-related stress."**
>
> *USA Today*

Be patient and kind to yourself. Don't expect miracles the first few times out of the box. Keep practicing. Like any new activity, it will start to feel natural over time. The benefits will be extraordinary. I'd suggest keeping a pen and pad or tape recorder nearby. After your alarm goes off and you open your eyes, write down the first few thoughts that come to your mind. Many of the most creative and unique ideas of my life have come to me after praying or meditating.

Be a Self-Esteem Addict

Why is self-esteem so crucial? The answer is simple. The way you choose to see yourself, virtually without exception, is also the way others will see you! Your self-image and self-esteem will affect the way you approach your goals, your career, your relationships, and your life. In order to succeed, you must first believe you deserve success and are capable of achieving success. Positive self-esteem is at the core of any program designed to make you successful at anything!

10 WAYS TO BUILD POSITIVE SELF-ESTEEM

- **Create positive self-esteem *internally.*** Look for the best in yourself. Look for traits and talents that make you unique. Make a list of your best qualities and carry it with you to remind yourself of your unique talents. Now sell those unique talents to others. Make them see and feel your uniqueness!

> **"The best things in life are yours, if you can appreciate yourself."**
>
> *Dale Carnegie*

- **Create positive self-esteem *externally.*** Like it or not, others make snap judgments based on the way you look and act. If you appear well-groomed, physically fit, confident, energetic, enthusiastic, and positive, others will find you attractive. They will see you as a leader. People will follow a leader! Make sure your external image reflects success and strength. Stand up straight, look others directly in the eye, smile often, and shake hands firmly. Make sure you are in superior physical shape—eat healthy foods and exercise often. When you look and feel the best of your life, you will automatically project a positive atti-

> **"Nobody can make you inferior without your consent."**
>
> *Eleanor Roosevelt*

tude! Above all, dress for success; it works! Make sure your clothes, car, and office all project an image of success, wealth, and power.

- **Look for ways to make others feel good about themselves.** Do you remember President John F. Kennedy? JFK did one thing very well: He was so positive and exuded so much confidence, that he made the country as a whole feel good! Americans felt confident in our country, our leader, and ourselves. JFK was so good at making us feel good, it is the only thing people remember about his presidency! There is a valuable lesson to be learned from this example: People want to feel good about themselves! It is intoxicating to feel positive about ourselves—to feel invincible. If you can make others feel that way, you are on your way to achieving success in any field you choose!

- **Educate yourself.** Education without confidence or a positive self-image guarantees nothing! But lack of education, combined with a poor self-image, virtually guarantees failure. With knowledge, no one can ever make you feel inferior! If you can combine a solid education, superior knowledge in your chosen field, and a positive self-image, you've created an unbeatable combination. Be open-minded—commit to expanding your knowledge for the rest of your life. Keep learning until the day you take your last breath!

- **Be prepared.** Stress and fear cause insecurity and negativity. But preparation destroys fear and builds confidence. If you have done your homework and are prepared for any possible scenario, you will enter into any situation with confidence and enthusiasm.

- **Make yourself feel good!** Congratulate yourself when you successfully surmount obstacles, make progress toward difficult goals, and even when you achieve smaller goals along the way. Spend a few moments each day reflecting on the blessings and good fortune in your life. Just as you tried hard to discover the things in your life that make you unique, here I ask you to work hard to find the things in your life that you should be thankful for. Make a list of all your good fortune and blessings. Whenever you catch yourself feeling depressed or angry, review this list to remind yourself of all the good things in your life! Remember, positive people always see the glass as half full!

- **Donate your time and money to others less fortunate.** Nothing will make you feel better about yourself than giving to others. And it will help you to put your priorities in order—you'll be better able to understand the pain and misfortune of others and therefore better able to recognize the blessings in your own life.

- **Build health with a positive and healthy lifestyle.** It's impossible to feel good about yourself or to project a positive self-image if you look sick or unhealthy! Most of us destroy health and energy with the foods we eat and a self-destructive lifestyle: junk foods, alcohol, smoking, drugs, lack of sleep and exercise. One of my most integral Positive Addictions is healthy living—eating healthy and exercising. Start scheduling exercise "appointments" into your busy day. Stay committed to a healthy lifestyle. Sign a contract with yourself—you are now contractually obligated!

- **Surround yourself with positive friends.** Find role models, mentors, and friends who will encourage you and inspire you. Watch them and learn from them. Copy them. Friends can either help and empower you every step of the way, or else they can drag you down. To succeed, you need to feel success, see success, breathe success, touch success, and smell success twenty-four hours a day. It must be part of your soul. You can't afford to be distracted by people who are jealous, bitter, or small. You need to see the possibilities—not the limits. Be careful who you choose to spend your time with. Find individuals who are on the same wavelength as you. You'll need their support, encouragement, and wisdom every step of the way!

- **Face your fears.** Failure has very little to do with playing the game and losing. The only real failure is never playing the game in the first place. Those afraid of risk are automatically failures. Make a list of your biggest fears and how they've held you back in life. Then decide how you could overcome those fears. Once you've faced a fear for the first time—win or lose—you'll feel exhilaration. It will set a pattern in motion—you'll gain so much confidence, you'll start to eagerly face all your fears. Success is like a snowball—once you've had a little, the rest builds and builds. Soon you're fearless and expecting success at everything you do!

Be an Affirmation and Visualization Addict!

> **"The empires of the future are the empires of the mind."**
>
> *Winston Churchill*

As you work to build positive self-esteem, you may find that some of your most critical obstacles are mental or emotional rather than physical: "I just can't see myself doing this," or "I doubt that I can really get out of the rut I'm in." Here I provide you with two powerful tools for overcoming those mental and emotional blocks—two ways to reprogram yourself for success.

These tools are crucial to developing positive self-esteem because they enable you to give yourself new, positive, success-oriented messages in place of the negative, failure-focused messages you may now be sending yourself. The first tool, affirmation, is a way to give yourself verbal messages that support your success. The second, visualization, helps you create a picture for yourself of how your successful life will look— to see yourself turning your dream into a reality!

Using affirmation and visualization allows you to create a new internal reality for yourself—as the first step in making that reality happen externally. These tools will create a success consciousness within you—a mental and emotional climate that supports and nurtures your successful self. You will see and feel your success—and what you see, feel, and believe happens! You will become that positive new you—someone that everyone can love and respect.

> **"As a man thinketh in his heart, so is he."**
>
> *Proverbs 23:7*

AFFIRMATIONS

First become aware of the negative messages you are sending yourself. Most of us have a constant low-level murmur going on deep inside the recesses of our brain. Unfortunately, this murmur is usually pretty negative. If you really concentrate on what your subconscious mind is telling you, you'll probably hear things like: "Come on, you'll never be able to accomplish that!" "That's a pipe dream—you're not smart enough to achieve that." Or "Someone like you doesn't deserve success." Becoming aware of how you bully yourself and promote your own failures is the first step toward changing.

Your second step is to create alternative positive messages. These are called affirmations. They are the antidote to that low-level negative murmur going on in your mind. You're now going to reprogram your subconscious to think positive. You will repeat these positive messages again and again—to recondition your subconscious mind. Let me give you a few examples:

- I am a success.

- My life is dedicated to being the best I can possibly be.

- I choose to be one of life's winners.

- Anything I can conceive, I can achieve.

- I have all the energy and enthusiasm I need to succeed.

- I am no longer a victim or a survivor, I am a THRIVER!

- Every day in every way, I move closer and closer to my dream.

- I can move mountains with my tenacity, commitment, enthusiasm, and determination.

- I will never give up. I am a fighter. My goal is to (fill in the blank) _____and I will not rest until I've turned my dream into a reality.

- My energy, enthusiasm, and spirit inspires others.

- I am a THRIVER. I surmount the insurmountable; I make the impossible possible.

- Every time I am rejected, I move that much closer to hearing the word *yes*.

- I will dream big, plan big, risk big, fail big, and finally succeed big!

These are just a few examples of affirmations. You must create your own personalized versions. Write sentences and sayings that resonate with your personality and your personal dreams and goals.

Now comes the third step—start repeating your personalized affirmations in front of a mirror. Look right

> **"The greatest discovery in one hundred years is the discovery of the power of the subconscious mind."**
>
> *William James*

into your eyes—feel your intensity, drive, and burning will. You are creating a new attitude, a new you, and a new future! As you repeat your affirmations each morning and/or night (for about two to five minutes at a time), you will notice a kind of rebellion. Just as when you first meditated, your mind will try to distract you and gain back control. It doesn't want to give up authority to you. You'll hear it answering your affirmations: You'll say out loud "I have all the energy and enthusiasm to make my dreams come true." Your mind will respond "Who are you kidding? You're the laziest, weakest, least motivated person around." Just let that negative thought drift by—don't even give it credence by paying attention to it. Simply repeat your positive affirmation. The more you repeat your affirmations, the weaker and weaker that subconscious murmur will become. After a dozen or so affirmations, your mind will give in and accept your new positive outlook—at least for now. You may need to reinforce your new positive outlook by repeating these same affirmations daily for weeks, months, or even years. Some of us have so much negative chatter, we'll need to use positive reinforcement for the rest of our lives. Others can get by with an affirmation session once a week or twice a month. You may also find that from time to time, it will be helpful to redo your personal affirmations—to reflect changes in the direction of your thinking, goals, and life.

VISUALIZATION

Now we come to the second half of this powerful one-two self-esteem punch—visualization. Affirmation utilized the power of verbal messages to reprogram your mind for success. Here, visualization utilizes the power of visual messages to accomplish the same goal. It has been said that "a picture is worth a thousand words." Actually, as far as your future success is concerned, it may be worth hundreds of thousands of dollars! Visualization is the process of seeing your success before you achieve it. Imagination is crucial to positive attitude. You've simply got to be able to see good things happening to you in your mind, before you start attracting those positive opportunities and situations. By visualizing good things, you start to believe in them and finally you start to really attract them.

> **"Your imagination is the preview to life's coming attractions."**
>
> *Albert Einstein*

How do you visualize? It's easy. First you sit in a comfortable and quiet place, free of distractions. The more relaxed you are, the more powerful the image you are able to create in your mind's eye. Next you create a picture of yourself in the situation you desire. Be as specific as you can. See the objects, companions, clothing, activities as you want them to be. It's like watching your own personal movie or television show. Make believe you're watching yourself in that show.

Now sit comfortably for two to five minutes, "acting" out the scene. Create as many details as possible—bring in all your senses. See the pattern on the jacket and tie you are wearing. See the expressions on the faces of your business associates or friends. See and hear your reaction to the conversation. See the detail in the table you are sitting at. Touch the ocean air at your beachfront home. Smell the new leather in the Jaguar you are driving. The more realistic your visualization, the more easily your mind will begin to believe that this situation really exists!

> **"Imagination rules the world."**
>
> *Napoleon Bonaparte*

After you've added all the details you can to your visualization, simply enjoy the internal experience you've created for yourself. After you're done, you'll feel energized, refreshed, and confident. Remember, your mind thinks you've just lived this experience. Let this daily visualization vacation inspire you to make the changes—large or small—that will move you forward toward the life of your dreams!

Step 2: Do It Today!

POWER PRINCIPLES

The Discipline Principle

Now to the centerpiece of my whole program. You can be the brightest person on the planet. You can possess the greatest ideas. You can shoot for the highest goals. But without discipline, you will never carry out those goals. Without discipline, all the commitment, confidence, and tenacity in the world is for naught. You can dream big dreams—but without discipline, that's all they'll ever be! Occasionally, individuals without discipline succeed—but their success is usually fleeting. They wind up losing it as quickly as they achieved it.

Discipline wins wars. Discipline keeps soldiers alive on battlefields. That's why armies since the beginning of time have been based on discipline. But why? What do sit-ups, push-ups, and ten-mile jogs have to do with success on the battlefield? What do spit-shined shoes and spotlessly-clean barracks have to do with winning wars? What do physical fitness and personal grooming habits have to do with courage and valor? The answer is everything! A disciplined soldier will be better focused, better organized under fire, better able to cope with life and death challenges. A disciplined soldier will be better prepared to think creatively under adverse conditions. A disciplined soldier will react like

> **"Discipline is the clear difference between having a dream, and living your dream!"**
>
> *Wayne Allyn Root*

a professional while others run for their lives—he or she will show courage and valor under intense fire. A disciplined soldier will automatically feel better about him or herself—show more confidence and pride. That automatically translates to tenacity, loyalty, and commitment—even in the midst of the most adverse conditions. War is a test, a test of a soldier's ability to think and perform when facing challenge and adversity. Like life, it isn't a question of whether you'll face challenge, adversity, and failure—it is only a question of how much you'll face and how you'll react. Discipline is what determines your reaction in the face of negativity, fear, and failure.

The modern world we all live in today very much resembles a battlefield. We all face tremendous stress and challenge on a variety of fronts. Raising healthy children is a daily battle. So is keeping a marriage together. The business world is a battlefield—getting to the top is like fighting a war! The landscape is littered with the casualties of the dead and wounded—the unemployed, the homeless, the bankrupt, the emotionally scarred. Like it or not, life is like battle—it is a daily test of your will. A battle for survival of the fittest. You will fight this battle every day of your life. Every time you walk into a job interview, every time a client auditions your firm or a customer walks into your store, every time you walk into a party looking for Mr. or Ms. Right—you are being tested. You are in a competition. Only the most disciplined will win. Only the best of the best will THRIVE!

The Planning Principle

No matter what stage you are at now, your journey cannot begin without goals! You've got to plan your future. You've got to figure out precisely where you are now, where you want to be tomorrow, and how you will get there. Nothing else can begin without this first step. There's an ancient proverb that sums up my point: "A journey of a thousand miles begins with one step." The Planning Principle is all about creating the life of your dreams by figuring out how, when, and where to take that first step. The Planning Principle is all about goals.

Why are goals so important? Would you attempt to drive from Boston to Los Angeles without a map? What about less familiar territory—would you cross the Sahara Desert without a map? Would you build your dream home without a blueprint? Would you practice shooting a gun at a target range without targets? I hope not—how could you hit anything, if you don't even know what you are aiming at? Would your family feel safe and secure if you died without a will? What would their future be like?

When you think of the great achievements in history, goals have been there every step of the way!

My first example of goals is the Constitution of the United States of America. The Constitution was a blueprint—a foundation designed by our founding fathers—a kind of vision for our future set down in writing by a group of the wisest men who ever lived. It worked through a civil war; through two world wars; through riots and civil rights protests; through the war on drugs and the war on urban crime; through the Vietnam War. Through thick and thin, America has been tested—it has bent— but it has never broken! Our country—despite all its problems—has remained the oldest and greatest example of democracy in the history of civilization. Why? Because we had a set of goals and rules to abide by. Because we had a vision to adhere to. A future mapped out before our eyes. A contract signed by our forefathers. The greatest contract ever written!

My second example is the Bible—a religious blueprint for the ages. The Bible is literally a set of goals and rules for all of mankind. The Bible—like our Constitution—is a grand vision of our future set down in writing by some of the great thinkers of all time. No, it's not perfect in the eyes of everyone. But in the final analysis, it is an extraordinary success. What other institution—besides religion—has survived thousands of years? And today there is a religious revival—an awakening that is attracting tens of millions formerly estranged from their faiths back to the fold.

Within the Bible is another religious blueprint, the Ten Commandments—again, a set of written goals that mankind has adhered to for thousands of years. And while many in society choose to break these rules every day, the Ten Commandments have formed the foundation of the rules of conduct that have governed civilized society for generations.

My fourth example is America's war efforts during World War II. After the bombing of Pearl Harbor,

President Franklin D. Roosevelt brought our nation together in the greatest war effort ever undertaken. We produced and manufactured more supplies and goods than any country in any war effort before or since. How? FDR challenged our nation with a set of goals and a shared sense of sacrifice. Those same goals won the war and preserved democracy and freedom.

Another grand example is the American space program. Another great leader and goal-setter, President John F. Kennedy, set a goal to put an American astronaut on the moon. That dream seemed so far away, so grandiose—some called it a "pipe dream." But JFK made the dream seem real, seem doable. He challenged us as a nation to aim high, sacrifice, and contribute as a team to stay committed to our goal. Despite setbacks, including the death of a crew of Apollo astronauts, a few short years later, Americans were walking on the moon. The impossible became possible! Goals were what enabled us to take those giant steps for mankind.

Goals are at work in the charity world, too! Think of the United Way and its goals—"tote-boards" set up in cities across America with red markers indicating how much money has been raised—until all the goals are met! And then there's the Muscular Dystrophy Telethon hosted each Labor Day by Jerry Lewis. What is the most memorable aspect of this annual ritual? Jerry Lewis asking for a drum roll and showing the "tote-board" every hour or so—to see if his goals have been met. The suspense of

"Luck is the residue of design."

Branch Rickey

comparing moneys raised to the annual goal is what has made this telethon such a huge success. More than just a success—it is part of American culture: Labor Day is now synonymous with the Jerry Lewis Telethon.

That's why goals are so important—they show you the way. They help you to stay on course when things are going badly. They light your path when it turns dark and ugly. They give you something to aim at, so you don't shoot yourself in the foot or run around in circles for a decade or two. Goals are your personal map, your personal blueprint, your personal foundation, your personal target—all wrapped up in one!

How important are goals? A recent study comparing people with goals versus those without found that those with goals earned over twice as much! That's double the income! And they did it by designing and reviewing their goals less than ten minutes a day! Can you spare a few minutes per day to double your income?

The Action Principle

When I think of action, I often think of a favorite story of mine. It's the story of a man with a strong faith in God. This man lives in a town where torrential rains are inundating the streets. Floodwaters are rising. A state of emergency has been called. Finally, a mandatory evacuation is ordered. Everyone is running for their lives. But not our faithful friend. He will not go. He tells his friends and neighbors that he has faith and he will not run. "God will protect me," he says.

So the town is evacuated. Only our friend stays behind. After a day, rescuers paddle to his home in a rowboat to ask him once again to evacuate. But he won't go—he says, "I have faith. I will be fine." On the second day the rescuers paddle out in the rowboat again. Again he won't budge. By the third day the rowboat is back again. Although he's now on his roof because of the rising waters, our faithful friend still won't go. On the fourth day rescuers find his body floating in the water.

The scene now shifts to heaven. Our faithful friend stands before God. He is angry and bewildered. "Why, why?" he asks God. "Why me? I was the only one with faith. How could you let me drown?" God replies, "What more could I do? I sent you three rowboats!"

The point of the story is that faith may be a foundation for successful living, but only if combined with action. Have you heard the wise saying, "God helps those who help themselves"? Action is the way to activate God. Goals are powerful tools, but without action they are meaningless. Faith is powerful, but without action it too is powerless. Energy and enthusiasm are powerful principles, but without action they are useless. You must get up off your couch, get out from under your bedsheets, get out from in front of the television, and take action! Action is what will change your life. Just the simple step of doing something seems to energize your life. Action equals power! By taking action, you make things happen. By making things happen, you create opportunity. And opportunity creates possibility.

And I've already explained possibility—if it's possible, you can make it happen. It all starts with action!

The greatest example of the power of the Action Principle belongs to our dear family friend Helen Andreeff. Helen is the mother of my wife's best friend. Helen lived in the same town for over half a century—Hamilton, Ontario, in Canada. She was divorced and living the life of a couch potato when she made the decision to take action. As Helen herself puts it, "I wasn't just a 'couch potato'—my butt was the couch!" Helen had heard a few of my motivational seminars and she finally got the message. Helen decided to shake up her life. In three short weeks, she sold everything she owned and moved three thousand miles to Los Angeles! That's more than just action—that's gumption! But Helen had only just begun. She was still lonely, depressed, and unsatisfied with her life. You see, moving three thousand miles may take courage, but it doesn't solve all your problems. Often people in distress take their problems with them wherever they go.

So Helen took action again—with a new lifestyle! She started exercising and eating healthy. She took up golf. And then she and her daughter Starr designed a personal ad—that's right, I said a personal ad! Millions of single women bemoan the fact that the odds of getting struck by lightning are higher than of finding a good man to marry after age fifty. Instead of complaining, Helen took matters into her own hands. She did something to change her situation. She took control of her life. I am so proud of her—here was a woman who just would not be denied. I knew at that moment she was going to succeed—no one was going to stop Helen Andreeff!

In her personal ad, Helen described herself as "attractive, over fifty, and a golfer." Over a hundred of the most eligible men from all over Southern California responded! That's right—I said over a hundred men! And most were educated and successful—after all, they were golfers. Helen dated dozens of men over the next few weeks. She married the best one of the group! Helen and Mike have been married for over five years now. Instead of living alone in a cramped studio apartment, working at a job she despised, Helen today commutes between her two homes—one in Beverly Hills and the other on a beautiful golf course in Montana! She spends her time golfing, skiing, and enjoying life. Her husband Mike is a lawyer, doctor, accountant, and screenwriter!

Action dramatically changed Helen's life. It can change yours too! It doesn't cost anything. It just requires some gumption (or, as we call it in New York, chutzpah)! My advice is simple—if you don't like the circumstance or direction of your life—stop complaining, stop wallowing in pity, and do something about it!

The Passion Principle

In order to take action and succeed you will need passion, emotion, and enthusiasm. Passion is what defines a THRIVER. THRIVERS love what they do! They inspire others to do the impossible. They are evangelists for their business, product, or cause!

Passion drives superachievers—THRIVERS. Find something you are passionate about and do it with all your might—with every fiber and cell in your being, with every bone in your body!

- When I think of music, I think of "The Chairman of the Board," Frank Sinatra; "The Hardest Working Man in Show Biz," James Brown; and of course Tina Turner, the most passionate singer ever to grace a stage! When I think of country music, I think of Garth Brooks. If you've never seen a Garth Brooks concert, you haven't seen passion. It's no coincidence these entertainers are some of the most successful entertainers in the history of the music business.

> **"Go after your dreams with such passion, such spirit, such determination, such intensity, that you'll either succeed or explode!"**
>
> *Wayne Allyn Root*

- When I think of conservative politics, I think of Newt Gingrich, Jack Kemp, and Rush Limbaugh. These men live and breathe their political passions. They believe so strongly in their causes that they bleed conservative politics. It takes leaders with their level of passion, intensity, conviction, and commitment to lead political revolutions! Whether you agree or disagree with their politics, these men define passion. And at the level of success they've achieved, what they do is unparalleled.

- On the other side of the political spectrum—liberal politics—I think of Hillary Clinton, Jesse Jackson, and in days past, Dr. Martin Luther King, Jr. Whether you agree or disagree with their brand of politics, these men and women define passion. Their passion and conviction has changed the world—even against insurmountable odds.

- When I think of great generals, I think of General Robert E. Lee, General George S. Patton, General Colin Powell, and General H. Norman Schwarzkopf ("Stormin' Norman"). These great leaders had passion for the men they led into battle. The result was exceptional performance from "their boys"—the soldiers they led into battle were overachievers. People respond to passion. Passion inspires soldiers to lay down their lives for their country!

- When I think of food, I think immediately of Martha Stewart, Julia Child, and Debbi Fields (Mrs. Fields, the "cookie queen"). These THRIVERS love food. They cook with passion. Their passion inspires others to create great meals too. They've made the world a better and tastier place because of their passions.

- When I think of opera, I think of Pavarotti. There's passion! And there—once again—is extraordinary success.

- When I think of passion for love, life, and children we all must think of Mother Teresa. She lives only to help and love those less fortunate. When I think of religion, I think of Dr. Robert Schuller and Rev. Billy Graham. These are men and women who have a passion for God, a passion for spreading the gospel, a passion for helping others. The result: Together they have empowered and comforted billions across the globe.

- When I think of presidents, I think of FDR, JFK, and Ronald Reagan. These were leaders whose passion was infectious. Americans felt proud to be Americans when these men sat in the White House. Another president, Abraham Lincoln, was the very definition of passion. You never had to ask Abe Lincoln which side of the fence he stood on—he gave his life for the principles he believed in.

- When I think of acting, I think of Robert DeNiro, Al Pacino, and Meryl Streep. Their passion lights up the screen. They are pure electricity.

- When I think of talk show hosts, I think of Oprah Winfrey. Here is a woman who cares about her audience—whose passion in life is enlightening and empowering the people who watch her show. Other hosts are interested in ratings and dollars. Oprah cares about educating others—improving the lives of others. She took a courageous stand against violence and dysfunction on her show. She paid for it with a temporary drop in ratings. Other hosts encouraged more violence and dysfunction to raise ratings. But in the long run, those hosts bit the dust. When the dust cleared, Oprah was left standing as the queen of talk shows! It's no coincidence she hosts the highest-rated talk show ever!

- When I think of sports, I think of many passionate athletes. It's no coincidence all achieved greatness. In basketball, there's Magic Johnson and Michael Jordan. In baseball, Babe Ruth, Reggie Jackson, and Pete Rose, A.K.A. "Charlie Hustle." In boxing, Muhammed Ali and George Foreman. In tennis, John McEnroe, Jimmy Connors, and Martina Navaratilova. In auto racing, Mario Andretti and A. J. Foyt. In football today, I think of Dan Marino. His fires burn deep. In years past, I think of Dick Butkus. In gymnastics, Mary Lou Retton defines enthusiasm and passion. These great athletes gave every ounce of blood they had to the sport they loved.

- When I think of passionate baseball managers, I think of Billy Martin, Earl Weaver, and Tommy Lasorda. They lived and breathed baseball. They were all winners. In football, there was Vince Lombardi, George Allen, and Don Shula. Football was their life! In basketball today, there's Pat Riley and Rick Pitino. They bleed hoops. Their passion for the game is unmatched. So is their success! In gymnastics, it's Bela Karoly.

- In business, I think of Donald Trump, Lee Iacocca, Ted Turner, H. Ross Perot, Jack Welch of General Electric, Herb Kelleher of Southwest Airlines, Richard Branson of Virgin Atlantic Airways, Bill

Gates of Microsoft, Jim Barksdale of Netscape Communications, and Steve Wynn of Mirage Resorts. Then there are the titans of the media world—Rupert Murdoch and Sumner Redstone. Though in their seventies, they still have more fire, more energy, more passion than men and women half their age. It's no wonder they are billionaires. These THRIVERS are masters at the game of business, because it is their passion in life—their reason for getting up in the morning. Look where passion has gotten them—these men are the "Who's Who" of American business history!

- When I think of exercise and diet gurus, I think of Jack LaLanne (a man who celebrates his birthday by pulling eighty rowboats filled with people through a harbor with his teeth definitely has passion) in the old days. Today I think of Richard Simmons, Tony Little, and Susan Powter. Their energy levels and passion levels are so high, you start moving to the beat just watching them! These television exercise gurus break windows and shatter glass with their level of intensity and fire! Their passion is contagious—that's why they are so successful: they pass on their passion to others through the television!

- Passion is even integral to lawyers. Think back to the O. J. Simpson trial. What were Johnnie Cochran, Marcia Clark, and Christopher Darden, if not passionate? A defendant's life was on the line. Nicole Simpson's children had lost a mother. Fred Goldman had lost a son. A justice system, a police department, and a famous athlete were all on trial—fighting for their lives. Did justice win? That's debatable. But passion won!

- When I think of passion in the computer world, I think of Guy Kawasaki of Apple Computer. Kawasaki is what can only be described as an "Apple Televangelist"! He travels the globe singing the praises of Apple computers, whipping packed houses of Apple fans into a frenzy, leading Apple in-house employee rallies, and trying to convert anyone not already on an Apple. He surfs the Internet trying to convert the world to Apple. The chairman of Apple calls Kawasaki a valuable "opinion leader." This passionate corporate cheerleader even posts a daily Mac newsletter on the Internet—appropriately called "EvangeList." It started with one thousand daily subscribers, but has quickly boomed to thirty-four thousand! Kawasaki understands that passion and spirit are more important to a company's survival than merely dollars and cents. He does his job so well that he even converted me! This book was written on Apple Computer products.

When I look back on my life, passion has driven me every step of the way. I have a passion for football and it led me—against all odds—to wind up on national television talking about football! I have a passion for motivating others and it has led you to read my book. I have a passion for healthy living (diet, exercise, prayer, vitamins) and now I'm able to share that passion with millions of others. I have a passion for family and faith in God and it has radically and dramatically changed my life. I live my life for my passions!

The Energizer Bunny Principle

The key to passion is energy. Without it, passion is virtually impossible. Energy fuels success. Energy is contagious. Energy is an aphrodisiac. Energy is valuable—actually it's priceless. Employers want to hire people with energy. People want to befriend people with energy. Law firms promote lawyers with energy to partners. Medical practices want to recruit young doctors with energy. Stock firms and investment banks earn hundreds of millions because of high-energy brokers and bankers. Lovers want to make love to people with energy. Clients want to hire people with energy to manage their accounts. Television producers are always looking for actors with energy and enthusiasm.

Energy is mysterious, exciting, exuberant, sexual, and intoxicating—like a wild stallion! Our modern, stressful, competitive world drains us of energy. So many of us fall by the wayside—tired and burned-out, drained of energy, passion, and enthusiasm. Once the

> **"Energy moves mountains. Energy awakens the dead. Energy frees the imprisoned. Energy defies the longest odds. Energy lights up the darkest path. Energy surmounts the insurmountable. Harness the energy inside you and gain the world."**
>
> *Wayne Allyn Root*

fire goes—the will to be the best—the rest of life goes. Without energy, it's over. Like it or not, fair or unfair, without energy you are out to pasture. But with that spark, that flame, that burning desire—you are in demand. You are hip, hot, and happening!

What exactly is energy? I believe it is a state of mind—an attitude. I call it the Energizer Bunny Principle. Have you ever seen the Energizer Batteries Bunny in television commercials? I have been called a living, breathing, human version of that famous bunny! That's the attitude I possess; my competitors, my critics, the naysayers—they can all laugh at me, shut doors in my face, shoot down my ideas, humiliate me, reject me, taunt me. They can even punch me, stomp me, kick me in the gut, hit me in the head with a lead pipe, shoot me, drop me in a river weighted down by concrete—but I just keep going and going and going! I am unstoppable! Believe me—an awful lot of people have tried. Once in a while they'll slow me down for a minute or two. But they can never stop me. I am relentless, tenacious, confident, committed, and above all, passionate! My energy is like ten thousand wild stallions. I cannot be tamed! Like that famous Energizer Bunny, I just keep going and going and going until my dreams are reality.

All successful people are high energy people. Why? Because life is trying. It is full of disappointment and failure, ups and downs. You will face doubters and naysayers. I guarantee you that from time to time. You will get knocked on your tail. And after a few years—

even a few decades of that kind of persistent pain—only those with the strongest will and the highest energy will survive and eventually thrive! That's why energy is so rare, so finite, and so valuable. That's why others are in awe of Energizer Bunnies. That's why they want to attach to you—they want to stand near you and share your power source. They live in darkness and they want to share your light—bask in your glow! It's a great feeling. It's a natural high to be around THRIVERS. It's exciting. It feels good! It feels powerful and intoxicating. it makes the pain go away.

The Motivation Principle

Motivation is what this book is all about! You've got to find a way to motivate yourself to be the best at whatever you do! Back in 1976, at the age of fourteen, I had my first motivation lesson. My friends and I were standing behind a large tree in my hometown of Mt. Vernon, New York, pelting cars with snowballs. Suddenly my eyes lit up. I saw a huge orange-colored garbage truck coming our way. It was like a giant neon sign—flashing "Hit me, hit me, hit me, please!" So I quickly packed up the hardest, heaviest snowball I could create! This was the "mother of all snowballs." Even then I understood the concept of the best. I was going to hit this huge garbage truck with the biggest, baddest, best snowball ever created! Just as the truck drove into my target zone, I ran out from behind the tree and let rip with the hardest throw of my life. Even today—twenty years later—the whole incident is still as clear as day in my mind. It all seemed to happen in slow motion. I can still see the snowball—which looked as big as a giant watermelon—floating toward the truck.

Suddenly my glee turned to horror as I realized it was going to hit a bull's-eye—right into the driver's window. It all happened in a split second—the realization that the driver's window was down and that the driver was going to be hit right smack in his face! I can still see his face so clearly. He was huge! His head was massive and he defined mean: huge arms on the steering wheel, angry scowl, dangling hoop earring, shaved head. He was a combination of Mr. Clean and Mr. T! This guy was bad news. I watched in horror as the snowball smashed into his skull. I stood paralyzed with fear for a moment and then watched as he stopped his huge truck and got out of his cab—blood running from his nose and lips—staring straight at me, with a look that could have melted all the snow in the neighborhood! I watched him reach into his front seat and pull out a metal pipe the length of a baseball bat. I was thinking a combination of three things: "This can't be happening to me!" "How did things get so out of hand?" and "I'm too young to die!"

And then he was charging toward me. It all happened so fast! I had been frozen in place for so long, he was already closing fast! At that moment, all I could feel was fear. I turned and ran—at a very young age I was already sensing what kind of situation I was facing here; this was not a joke or a little adolescent fistfight. I was facing death or a crippling beating at the hands of an enraged madman with a lead pipe. I knew immediately there was no reasoning, apologizing, or even begging with this madman. If he managed to catch me, he was going to hurt me badly. One look at his eyes and I knew that this man liked to hurt people. I had just triggered every ounce of pain and anger in his life. If I didn't run fast—I was going to pay with my life.

So I ran and ran and ran. I must have set New York state track records. But now my horror turned to disbelief, because in front of me stood a major highway—the Hutchinson River Parkway. And beyond that flowed the Hutchinson River. Keep in mind that it was a snowy, freezing, winter day. I was cold, scared, and motivated to the hilt: My motivation at that moment was clear—survival! I wanted desperately to live. I had to think fast and take positive action or die. There was no choice. I crossed a busy highway during rush hour. I dodged cars heading for me at sixty miles an hour in four lanes! I was almost hit twice. Several cars swerved or braked to avoid me and almost went off the highway.

I looked back and saw Mr. Clean crossing the highway too! I realized this was the defining moment of my life. I ran forward into the Hutchinson River and jumped in. It's amazing how effective adrenaline can be in moments like this. I disregarded the fact that I couldn't swim! The Hutchinson River was swollen from the snow, but it was still only chest high. Somehow I staggered across the river. It must have been just slightly above freezing, because it felt like ice. I found my way across the river and crawled onto the dirt bank on the other side. I was exhausted, freezing, shaking, and out of gas. I looked back and saw Mr. Clean looking across the river, cursing and screaming at me. I knew from the look on his face he wasn't going into the river. I had won! My will had been stronger than his. He stood on the other side of the river ranting, raving, and waving his lead pipe at me. I was in no mood to taunt him. I just watched his tirade in disbelief. I was grateful to God that I had survived. I watched him run back toward the highway. He crossed the highway again—and he seemed in a hurry. I suddenly realized my ordeal wasn't over. He was going to get his truck.

I ran toward the nearest houses. I hysterically knocked on a few doors but no one was home. Then I saw a big orange truck coming around the bend— with two giant legs walking slowly alongside. I dived under a car in one of the driveways. The snow was up to the tires, so I dug a cavern under the car. I was soaked from head to toe by my afternoon swim and now I was buried in snow under a car! I quickly and carefully dug a small hole to see out of. What I saw made me sick to my stomach: "Mr. Clean" walking a few feet away, alongside his truck (his partner was driving), with his trusty lead pipe in his hand. I covered the peephole and rolled up into a ball. There was no way for anyone to see me! I waited about an hour—it seemed like a day—and then crawled out and ran home, hiding behind every tree and telephone pole along the way.

In all the years before and all the years since, I have never again had reason to cross a busy highway or swim a frozen river. But that day, I dug down and found something deep inside of me. I became a goal-setter that day. I made my goal happen—I lived! I became a motivator that day too. I knew that if I could bottle the same motivation I had felt on that miserable day, I could accomplish anything I wanted to for the rest of my life! I've used the images of that day to motivate me again and again. Once again I managed to turn lemons to lemonade! That frightening incident will empower me and motivate me for the rest of my life!

Life comes down to motivation. And motivation comes down to desire and hunger—how badly do you want the goal? Do you want it more than the next guy? What are you willing to sacrifice to achieve your goals? What will it take to stop you? Those are the questions you've got to ask yourself every day. You've got to establish your goals, then find out what it will take to make them happen, and finally determine your level of desire. What motivates you? What prize is so valuable to you that it will light that kind of burning desire deep down inside? Find that something, or create it in others, and the world is yours!

The Personal Responsibility Principle
This is a tough one to follow, but it's the first step necessary to enjoy the life of your dreams. Personal responsibility simply means "If it is to be, it is up to me." Your dreams are your responsibility. There are no

knights in shining armor, no sugar daddies, no invincible superheroes. You must stop blaming others for your failures and depending on others for some distant future success.

"If it's to be, it's up to me. My life is my responsibility!"

Wayne Allyn Root

Like it or not, we live in an age of shrinking budgets and eroding governmental authority. Government cannot and should not guarantee your livelihood. Corporations certainly won't either. You cannot depend on anyone providing you with cradle-to-grave support. You can't even count on family—your own mother and father may be struggling to survive a retirement future dependent on a spartan or bankrupt Social Security system.

Your job is to develop the mind-set of a THRIVER. Create a clear set of goals. Create a realistic game plan. Prepare for worst-case scenarios. Stop complaining. Stop watching television. Educate yourself. Empower yourself. Take credit and responsibility for your problems and failures. Don't be jealous of what others have achieved. Be happy for them and intently set your sights on what you can achieve! Practice a disciplined way of life. Practice long range vision—take advantage of the trends of the future by opening a small business or home-based business. Put your future in your own hands. Only *you* are responsible for you! From this day forward, you are now the master of your own destiny

POSITIVE ADDICTIONS

Be a Discipline Addict!

The most precious commodity in our modern society isn't money, happiness, health, or fulfillment. It is time. Time is priceless. We never have enough of it! If each of us had more time, we'd automatically make more money, we'd automatically enjoy life more, we'd automatically enjoy better relationships with those we love, and we'd be healthier (we could cook and enjoy natural, healthy meals instead of scarfing fast food, junk food, and TV dinners)! That's why you must become addicted to discipline.

To get in tune with yourself—to become more spiritual, more creative, more energetic, more enthusiastic, more confident, more focused, more tenacious, more committed, more fulfilled, even healthier—you will need to be highly disciplined. You will need to keep detailed track of every minute of every day. You will need to plan religiously your day from morning to night. And you will need to stay committed to this plan without exception. You will even need to sign a contract with yourself to ensure your dedication to this plan of action!

The point of all this discipline, planning, and organizational zeal is to ensure that you set aside the time necessary to do the things in your life that produce success, attract opportunity, and encourage personal growth. We all set aside the time to go to school or work. We set aside the time to go to the dentist, eye doctor, or veterinarian. We set aside the time to take our kids to school, ballet lessons, and Little League. We set aside the time to do business. Most of us have important business meetings and appointments set up all day long. Those who are successful at business stick to them. Many of us are so busy, we even need to set appointments to spend time with our spouses and families! Most of us plan our annual or semiannual vacations far in advance. Why? Why do we set all these appointments down in writing (on a calendar, in a business diary or daily planner)? Because if we didn't set a specific time for school, work, business meetings, doctor visits, dates with our spouse, or even vacations, we'd never get to them. But because they are scheduled and planned, we make it our business to perform: to be there at a set time and place and take action. It is obvious that in order to achieve our goals, we need to plan out our lives to the most minute detail.

Well, why don't we set our personal and spiritual goals down in writing? Why don't we plan our personal growth? Why don't we plan the activities that will change our lives and empower our futures? Why don't we plan success? From this day forward you will!

Success is all about setting aside the time to pray every day, to meditate, to affirm, to visualize, to organize, to goal plan, to exercise, to eat healthy and live healthy, to energize, to think positive, to appreciate the blessings in your life, and to spend with your family and the people you love. Your job is to schedule appointments with yourself each day to make sure these activities get done. These activities are more important to your success, health, and well-being than any business meeting or dental appointment. How do you become a discipline addict?

- **First and foremost, get up early each and every day!** Remember the saying, "The early bird catches the worm"? It's true! Make it a regular part of your regimen to get up early each day and get a jump on life! I credit much of my success to the fact that I get more done by 10:00 A.M. than most people do in an entire day. The people I know who get up late in the day are usually hiding from their fears. Getting up late is a way of avoiding the things in life you are afraid of—facing a job you dislike, a career going nowhere, a failing relationship, or responsibilities you cannot or will not live up to. The people I know who are THRIVERS literally bound up out of bed at the crack of dawn—eager and enthusiastic to face the day ahead. They look forward to the challenges of life and the opportunity to surmount those challenges. They know that today is the first day of the rest of their lives. No matter what yesterday was like, they understand that today is a brand-new opportunity to improve their lives! Their lives are dominated by energy and enthusiasm—not pessimism, depression, and anxiety. Getting up early is a disciplined way of turning energy and enthusiasm into opportunity and success! If you're having trouble getting up earlier, set your alarm clock to wake up one minute earlier each day for two months. It doesn't sound like much, but at the end of sixty days, you've gained an extra hour. At the end of four months, you've gradually gained two hours! Experiment and adjust according to your personal goals.

- **Face your fears—write them all down.** Schedule time each day to deal with your fears, change them, or surmount them. If you ignore them, they will not go away. They will fester and magnify. If you deal with them—face to face—you will feel a tremendous sense of relief and optimism that will envelop everything else you do throughout your day. The confidence and positive self-esteem that comes from tackling difficult issues will give you the confidence to achieve any goal you set in life for the rest of your life!

- **Eliminate procrastination. Become a list maniac.** Make lists of everything you need to accomplish today (ultra-short term), this week (short term), this month (medium term), and this year (long term). Then do it—now! Don't put anything off until later or, like most people on this planet, you will never get it done! Follow the list—in order—from top to bottom. Anything you can't finish on today's list, move onto tomorrow's list. If it doesn't get done tomorrow, move it to the next day or the next day or the day after that. Keep it on your "to do" list until it gets done—period!

- **Schedule out every fifteen minutes of your day.**
  Have a detailed plan for what you will be doing,
  where you will be going, and what you want to
  accomplish today. No, I'm not out of my mind—I realize you'll never keep to a schedule that tight. But
  what does this schedule represent? It is a daily goal.
  People with goals accomplish so much more than
  people without. Now you have detailed daily time
  goals. That doesn't mean I expect you to meet all
  these goals, but what if you meet some of them? If
  you simply meet a few of your goals each day, you'll
  enjoy a dramatic improvement in your efficiency
  level, success level, and time management level. The
  result will be a whole new quality of life!

- **Schedule daily appointments for your exercise,
  prayer, meditation, goal planning, affirmation,
  visualization, and other integral daily activities.** If you don't plan them, they won't get done.
  These Positive Addictions are your most important
  daily activities. You will need them to face the day
  ahead with energy, enthusiasm, focus, creativity, and
  confidence. Yet without a detailed list of appointments for each activity, they'll get put off, pushed
  forward, or forgotten. There is nothing in your life
  more important than scheduling time for the habits
  that lead to success, energy, and sanity!

- **These are your rules.** Every day starts and begins
  with push-ups, sit-ups, and yoga stretching exercises.
  Then a brisk walk or a jog. All of these activities are

free. They cost you nothing. But they pay off big-time in energy, self-esteem, goal setting, confidence, and enthusiasm. You must also pray and meditate. Period. These activities are also free—they cost you nothing. But the payoff in your ability to focus and enjoy deep personal fulfillment is priceless! You may or may not get to every Positive Addiction on your schedule. But the three that make up the foundations of your day—prayer, meditation, and exercise—are your musts! To ensure a dedication to these "musts" of your new program, sign a contract with yourself and "post" it on your bathroom mirror. Each morning it will be staring you in the face as soon as you awaken. You are now contractually obligated!

- **Schedule your TV time.** I'd like you to shut off your television altogether. But realistically, that's not going to happen. Instead, let's compromise. Pick seven to ten hours a week you really enjoy. Now schedule those viewing hours into your week. Build the rest of your schedule around these blocks of set-aside TV time. With all the extra time you've freed up for yourself, you now have the freedom and flexibility to schedule family time, exercise, education (read inspiring biographies or study for a new degree), or that hobby or second career you've never had time for. You now have no excuses left—it's time to change your life!

- **Set aside time each day for action.** Go "Rolodex surfing"! Leave a "window" each week to contact people who might help your career or buy your products. Look up old friends, business acquaintances, or old clients (in your Rolodex or business phone book) whom you haven't heard from in a long while. Rekindle these relationships. Mail or fax them updates on your career, company, or product. When you run out of old contacts to rekindle, use that weekly window to find new ones! Never sit idly by. The only way to progress is to promote change, to constantly add new clients, investors, partners, and customers to the mix. The same concept works with relationships—never sit idly by and complain. Take action. Cultivate new relationships! You have no right to complain unless you are out there fighting in the trenches! And if you're doing that, you won't have time to complain!

• **Discipline extends to all areas of your life, even your home.** Set a goal to keep your home clean and uncluttered. Discipline is like tenacity—you either are disciplined all the time or you're not. Keep your home spotless and uncluttered. Soon your life, career, and relationships will be as well. A messy, dirty, unkempt home will turn into a messy, unkempt life! Your goal is now to envelop all areas of your life in the principles of discipline and organization.

I don't waste a second of my precious time. Everything is planned and detailed. I know what I have to do and I do it! Yes, I am a marine drill sergeant, but I'm a happy one, a healthy one, and a wealthy one! My program works! I need to live my life with passion. So do you! I need to live my life with discipline, organization, and order. So do you! I need to live my life by my Power Principles. So do you! I need to live my life addicted to my Positive Addictions. So do you! Discipline makes it all happen!

Be a Goal-Planning Addict!

Now it's time to plan the life of your dreams. To do that you need a target—something to aim at. How can you hit a target if you don't know what you are aiming at? By answering the following questions honestly and accurately, you can begin to assess your life, your goals and dreams, and the obstacles that stand in your way. Only then can you design a game plan to turn those dreams into realities!

Goal-Planning Activities:

In order to create a better future, you must first understand your past.

A The Past

- Am I satisfied with my past financial state?

- Am I satisfied with the direction of my past relationships?

- Am I satisfied with my past physical state (state of health)?

- Am I satisfied with my past emotional state?

- Am I satisfied with my past spiritual state?

- If I am unhappy, why?

- What has been holding me back in the past?

- Were others to blame for my past difficulties?

- What was my role in these difficulties?

- What can I learn from my past problems, pain, and failures?

- I take personal responsibility for:

- If I had to do it over again, I'd handle things this way:

- I wronged the following people and I'd like to apologize to them:

> **"Plan your work for today and everyday, then work your plan."**
>
> *Norman Vincent Peale*

- I will seek out and offer restitution to the following people:

- In the past, I handled stress in the following ways:

- In the past, I handled fear in the following ways:

- In the past, I handled the word *no* in the following ways:

- In the past, I attracted the following kinds of situations, opportunities, and relationships:

- In the past, in response to challenge, adversity, and rejection, I chose to become addicted to:

- It is said, "History repeats itself again and again." I will take the following steps to see that I do not repeat these same mistakes:

B The Present

- The following is a list of my talents and positive traits:

- The following is a list of my weaknesses and short-comings:

- The following is a list of the things I like about my life, job, or career today:

- The following is a list of the things I do not like about my life, job, or career today:

- The following is how I'd describe my financial state at this moment:

- The following is how I'd describe my emotional state at this moment:

- The following is how I'd describe my physical state at this moment:

- The following is how I'd describe my spiritual state at this moment:

- The following is how I'd describe the present relationships in my life:

- Would I be fulfilled living the life I'm living today for the rest of my life?

- If not, here is what I propose doing about it:

- Here are the changes I'd have to make in my life to start living the life of my dreams:

- What is preventing me from making those changes?

- Are my friends or family standing in my way?

- Are my energy and enthusiasm levels high enough to change my life?

- Are my self-esteem and confidence levels high enough to make the changes necessary in my life?

- Do I have a self-destructive personality? When things are going well in my life, here is how I react:

- Here are the things I fear most in life:

- These are the fears that stand in the way of the life of my dreams:

- These are the obstacles that stand in my way:

- Here is how I might overcome those obstacles:

- These are the attitudes, habits, traits, ideas, and principles I'll need to institute in order to move forward:

- This is what my typical day is like:

- This is what I'd like my typical day to look like:

- Who are my role models?

- Who are my mentors?

- What could I do to live my life more like them?

- What are my values?

- Would I like to change my values?

- What are my passions?

- What would it take to create more passion in my life?

- How do my friends, family, and business associates fit into the big picture?

- How would my friends and family be affected by positive changes in my life?

- If I could, what changes would I make in my choice of friends and relationships?

- Deep down, do I think I deserve success?

- Deep down, do I believe in my ability to make my dreams come true?

- Do I have negative thought patterns? Is there a constant negative chatter going on in my subconscious?

- What is my negative thought pattern saying?

- What could I do to change my thought pattern?

- How do I define myself today?

- How do I think others define me?

- What could I do to change that definition?

- What aspects of my physical appearance (pale, tan, fat, thin, bald, long hair, hair color, muscular, face, body, etc.) bother me?

- Do I believe any aspects of my physical appearance have hindered my career, personal, or professional relationships?

- Do I believe any aspect of my physical appearance has hurt my self-esteem?

- How could I change the physical limitations or imperfections that bother me or others?

- How would those changes affect my life?

- What separates me or the products/skills I sell from my competition?

- What material things do I need to improve my current career or financial state? (i.e. computer, tools, cell phone, fax, pager, nicer office, new car, better clothes, briefcase, jewelry, etc.)

- What's standing in my way of obtaining these things?

- How could I overcome these obstacles?

C The Future

In order to turn your dreams into reality, you have to first allow yourself to dream. This activity will give you a chance to decide what it is you really want.

Dreams can be wild, or true, or some of both. A wild dream is one which is beyond your control and has little chance of happening—a five-foot, eight-inch tall man wanting to be a pro basketball player, for instance, or a woman who's tone-deaf longing to be an opera singer. (It's okay to dream those dreams, though, because they may lead you to the true dreams that you can fulfill.) Right now, write down one or two of your wild dreams—if anything were possible, what would you want in your life?

Now for your true dreams.

What would you really like your life to be like, both personally and/or professionally? Can you fulfill some part of your wild dreams? For example, our five-foot, eight-inch tall man might dream of becoming a sportscaster, sports coach, sportswriter, or the owner of a sports memorabilia store; our tone-deaf woman might dream of directing the Opera Guild or becoming a music teacher. Right now, write down one or more true dreams—dreams you want to turn into reality.

Now try the same exercise after praying and meditating. First put on relaxing music. Set your timer for fifteen minutes. Close your eyes. Breathe in deeply. Hold. Breathe out slowly. Concentrate on each breath. Keep a notepad or tape recorder nearby. As soon as you awaken, answer the following questions:

- What do I really want out of life?

- How does that answer match up with the wild and true dreams I created before meditating?

- If I made my dream(s) come true, what would that give me? How would my life change?

- So based on that answer, could I revise my goals or dreams? What do I really want?

- How would I like to define myself tomorrow?

- How would I like to define myself in a few years?

- How would I like to define myself in ten years? In twenty years?

- How would I like to be remembered? What would I like my obituary to say?

- What am I doing to create a new future for myself and my family?

- Based on where I am right now, what's most likely to stand in my way of achieving my goal(s)?
    Financially:
    Physically:
    Emotionally:
    Spiritually:

D The Game Plan

Take the obstacles and challenges listed above and design a game plan. Select doable actions you can take over the short and long term to overcome those obstacles and turn your dream(s) into reality. Write down each obstacle, your short-term action plan for overcoming it, and your long-term plan.

E A Specific Detailed Time Frame

The key to goal planning is to make your goals and dreams as specific and detailed as possible.

Put specific dates to all of your goals and dreams. These include financial dates, emotional dates, physical dates, and spiritual dates.

F Measure Your Progress

At regular intervals be sure to measure your progress. Make up a progress chart similar to this:

PROGRESS CHART

This Week	NONE	POOR	GOOD	EXCELLENT
My financial progress:	☐	☐	☐	☐
My emotional progress:	☐	☐	☐	☐
My physical progress:	☐	☐	☐	☐
My spiritual progress:	☐	☐	☐	☐

Additional notes on my progress:
This month:
In six months:
In one year:

G Failure and Rejection Exercises

No book called *The Joy of Failure!* would be complete without exercises aimed specifically at overcoming the fear of failure. Many of you are not progressing simply because you are afraid of failure and rejection. It's important that you understand how irrational those fears are. Try answering the following questions:

- Am I afraid of failure and rejection?

- Why?

- What are the three worst failures of my life?

- What are the three worst rejections of my life?

- After reading Wayne Root's story and the stories of other "successful failures," do my failures and rejections still seem so bad?

- How can I learn from failure and rejection?

- How has failure made me stronger in the past?

- What is the worst that can happen if I try and fail?

- What is the best that can happen if I try and succeed?

- What is the best that can happen, if I never try or risk in the first place?

- As I think of my life today, how can I turn lemons into lemonade?

- As I think of the Possibility Principle, are there areas in my life where I could make the impossible possible with a change in attitude and spirit?

- When the going gets tough and the odds seem insurmountable, what can I do to stay positive, motivated, and committed?

- Why do I think I bought this book? What do I hope to get out of this program?

◾H Creating Your Picture Planner

You have just taken what you want to achieve in life and put it to paper. You've utilized words to create a new future. Now I want you to utilize images—create a visual or picture planner for your subconscious.

- Comb through your favorite dream magazines: *Vogue, Cosmopolitan, GQ,* the *Robb Report, Forbes, Town & Country, Great Estates,* etc.

- Find images and pictures that resonate with you— that represent the life you want to live and the person you want to be in the future!
   The home(s) you want to live in
   The car(s) you want to drive
   The style you want to project
   The vacations you want to take
   The body you'd like to create for yourself
   The boat or plane you'd like to own
   The family or relationship(s) you'd like to build

- Find images or photos that represent happiness, health, and fulfillment to you.

- Now cut out all these images and photos. Buy a diary or photo album specifically for your picture planner. Paste or tape these photos into your personalized book. This is how your future will look! You now have your future in your own hands; you are in control of your own destiny!

• Take the time once or twice a week to browse through your picture planner. Then close your eyes and clearly visualize yourself in that house, in that car, in the elegant new office, on that wondrous trip with your happy, healthy family. The more detailed your visualization, the better.

• When you are done with your visualization say a prayer and thank God for the opportunity to see such beautiful and inspiring images. Thank God for the opportunity to turn your dreams into reality. Thank God for the freedom to create a new life for yourself!

• Finish up your exercise by saying out loud over and over again—"Whatever I can conceive, I will achieve!"

Our subconscious minds think in pictures or visual images. Our subconscious cannot differentiate between real and imagined. In other words, your mind believes what it sees. If you visualize success and happiness, your mind will reprogram itself to believe you are already enjoying success and happiness. That reprogramming will create a new you—happy, optimistic, positive, expecting success, and attracting new opportunities like a magnet! To actualize success, you must first visualize success.

> **"Believe in impossibilities; that which is impossible with man is possible with God."**
>
> *Norman Vincent Peale*

▌ Your Personal Contract

You've put your dreams down in words and pictures. Now it's time for the final step—you must sign a contract with yourself. A sample contract is on the following page. Agree to specific, personalized rules of attitude and conduct and specific dates. Remember, your word is your bond. Be honest—you can't cheat or lie to yourself. Review your contract often and analyze your progress. Update and amend. But always try to be true to your word.

Be a Motivation and Education Addict!

You must stay motivated and educated! In a competitive, dog-eat-dog business and sales world, you've got to find a way to stay on top of your game—to stay hungry, to know more than your competitors and customers.

Some of you will tell me that you are not in sales, so you don't need to be so competitive. You are mistaken. We are all in sales! Every time you go on a job interview, you are selling yourself! Every time your company or employer considers layoffs, you are in a sales position. If you're single, every time you walk into a bar or attend a party, you are in a sales position—you are selling yourself! Even if you have a challenging and rewarding job, you are selling yourself and your ideas to your boss, manager, co-workers, partners, and potential clients every single day. Life is sales! Here are a few ideas to keep you motivated:

MY PERSONAL CONTRACT

I, _____, agree on this _____ day of_____,
199__, that my long term goals are:_____
_____.
I agree that to make these goals a reality, I
must_____
_____.
I agree that I am committed fully to these goals. There
is no turning back!
This is a binding legal contract between me, myself,
and I.
I agree to be tenacious, energetic, enthusiastic, passionate, optimistic, disciplined, creative, and motivated.
I agree to have faith in my own power to make my
dreams come true.
I agree to stay positive and active in the face of obstacles,
challenges, and adversity. I agree to overcome anything
and anyone standing in my way.
I, _____, agree to achieve my goals by the
_____ day of _____ 199__. Nothing will stop me.
I am a card-carrying certified member of The Root
Revolution!
I am a THRIVER! I understand that there will be setbacks and failures along the way, but I am prepared to
fail my way to the top!
I am now contractually obligated to succeed!

Signed _____ Date_____

**Copyright © 1996 by Wayne Allyn Root and Root
International**

- Invest in biographies of great men and women of our time—individuals whose stories will inspire and energize you! You'll need positive role models—you won't find them on television. The next time the going gets tough or you get burned-out, turn to the life stories of people like Ben Franklin, George Washington, Abraham Lincoln, Golda Meir, Thomas Edison, General George Patton, General Douglas MacArthur, General Robert E. Lee, Sir Winston Churchill, Madame Marie Curie, Franklin D. Roosevelt, John F. Kennedy, Dr. Martin Luther King, Jr. When the going got tough, these great leaders got tougher. Their stories of triumph over adversity will never go out of style. Their attitudes and principles of success still apply today!

- Invest in newspapers and magazines that successful individuals read. Publications like *The New York Times,* the *Los Angeles Times, The Wall Street Journal, Forbes, Fortune, Barron's, Business Week,* and the *Robb Report.* I read all these publications to get inspired, to get educated, to spur my creativity, to learn the language of my role models—THRIVERS. They read these publications; if you want to THRIVE, so will you!

- Invest in motivational books and tapes. If you sell for a living—and in one way or another we all do— you'll need to lift your spirits and recharge your soul from time to time. Just as you invest a percent of your income in stocks and bonds each year and just as you contribute a certain percent of your income to charity annually, set aside a percentage toward motivational books and tapes. As you climb the ladder of success and earn more money, invest more in staying motivated—so you stay on top! If you own a business, invest in an inspirational library—a room in your company where employees can go to check out inspiring biographic and motivational books, video- and audiotapes.

> **"Knowledge is the food of the soul."**
>
> *Plato*

- Invest in a home gym. Or if you own a business, invest in a corporate gym where employees can go to work out at lunchtime. The payoff will be energy, enthusiasm, lower medical bills, reduced health insurance rates, and higher self-esteem!

- Invest in continuing education to stay on top of your game. Education is a lifetime process—it never ends. Challenge yourself to keep improving. Go back to college and add new degrees. Or take advantage of the newest wrinkle in education: accredited home-study classes and Internet courses leading to advanced degrees. Never stop learning, improving, educating, and advancing!

Step 3: Do It with Style!

POWER PRINCIPLES

The Healthy Living Principle

Now that you're in a good mood—feeling good about yourself and positive about the world you live in—it's time to elevate your body to the same level of fitness as your mind and spirit. A great philosopher once said that health is wealth. What he meant, of course, is that nothing is more important than your state of health and well-being. A healthy body is worth all the money in the world.

But to me there is a more direct correlation between health and wealth. I believe that good health actually produces wealth: physical fitness equals fiscal fitness! Nothing will help you to achieve success, wealth, or even power like a healthy body. I believe you must literally eat and exercise your way to the top! Chemicals, toxins, drugs, alcohol, and other poisons in the body will reduce your energy level, suppress your immune system, and cloud your creative abilities. A healthy diet and lifestyle produce the energy necessary to develop creative ideas, enable you to work long and productive hours, enhance concentration, and promote emotional balance and stability.

Success is all about teamwork and leadership. Healthy, high energy individuals inspire and motivate others. It's easy for people to get enthusiastic about going to work when they like the people they're working with! It's easy to get enthusiastic about that new project when one's co-workers are enthusiastic and excited. It's easy to develop a winning attitude working alongside a positive thinker.

An individual who eats right, drinks moderately, and exercises rigorously is also much more capable of dealing with high levels of stress. Success requires discipline and mental toughness. Exercise enthusiasts feel good about themselves because they have proven to themselves that when the going gets tough, they get tougher. They know what it's like to set personal records on days they didn't feel like getting out of bed. They know what it's like to conquer that mountain or run that last mile—even when their body is screaming *No!* That's why they set business records against insurmountable odds and surmount failure and rejection without hesitation. Exercise also helps you live by goals. Exercise enthusiasts run marathons or climb mountains one step at a time, until they reach the finish line or the mountaintop.

If I still haven't convinced you to switch to a healthy diet and lifestyle, maybe the promise of a better sex life will do the trick! A recent national study in *Redbook* magazine reported that exercise enthusiasts experienced increased sexual desire, increased sexual enjoyment, and more active sex lives! Yet another study reported that men who exercised vigorously enjoyed more active and satisfying sex lives.

> **"To lose one's health renders science null, art inglorious, strength unavailing, wealth useless, and eloquence powerless."**
>
> *Herophilus*

And the kind of exercise you choose doesn't matter! Studies centering on aerobics, weight training, swimming, jogging, and cycling all reported the same result: physical activity increases libido!

At this point you may still have one reservation— how do I do it? Many of you might be thinking that it is impossible to change your diet and lifestyle. Others may be thinking that it is impractical to fit a healthy lifestyle into a hectic, high-stress life. Finally, a good many of you may be high-energy Type A personalities. You may be thinking that Type A and healthy living go together like oil and vinegar. Wrong on all counts! A recent study of Type A's debunks that myth completely. Even the author of the study assumed that aggressive, competitive, adrenaline junkies would make poor candidates for a healthy lifestyle. In fact they made ideal candidates! Type A workaholics are driven, competitive, and goal oriented. Competitive Type A's set out to "out-health" their competition—and they do! Competitive desires, instead of working against adrenaline junkies, work in a positive way when applied to positive goals. The study proved that a can-do spirit is fantastic, as long as your goal is to create a positive, healthy lifestyle!

The Armani Principle

Here is one of the most powerful principles in my arsenal—and one of my personal favorites. You see, while God, family, and spirituality are integral foundations of my life—so is Giorgio Armani!

This integral principle is left out of the philosophy of most positive thinkers, spiritual leaders, and motivational speakers. They don't deal with life in the real world—I do! The truth is—whether you like it or not—people judge you by the way you look: your image. The way you look determines your value.

- Adults do it every day! Think of a hot new movie opening. A hot new restaurant. A hot new sports car selling for thousands over list price. Everyone wants what is perceived as valuable, special, or exclusive. If you tell people they can't have it—they want it. If you tell them they can't get in—they want in! It's human nature.

- It works with real estate. Trust me! I've learned the hard way that buyers don't care about plumbing, heating, air-conditioning, or septic systems. The value of a house is determined by how it looks to the naked eye—a fresh coat of paint, new floors, a new kitchen, shiny new bathroom fixtures.

- It works when you sell a car. If you have the greatest car in the world, but it hasn't been cleaned in a month—it's covered with dents and scratches outside and carpet stains inside—it will not sell! The exact same car in spotless condition will sell for top price, in record time!

- It works in the corporate world. Companies like Xerox, Federal Express, and MCI have spent tens of millions of dollars in the last few years to change their corporate logos. Why? Because a logo is the first thing you notice about a company. Your first impression could determine whether you buy from that company or not. It is sad but true—your product might be inferior, but people will still buy it if the outside package is attractive.

- It happens every day in the fashion world. Billions of dollars are spent on clothing and makeup modeled by beautiful people, who just happen to make the clothes and makeup they are wearing look great! If the people modeling the clothes looked unsuccessful, unsexy, unkempt, unattractive, or mentally ill, do you think you'd buy the clothes? Do you think anyone would?

- It even works in sports. Pat Riley is one of the winningest coaches in the history of sports. His success is built around image. He believes that if you look like a million bucks, you'll play like a million bucks! Among his first acts as head coach of the Miami Heat: upgrading the image of the team! He convinced the owner of the Heat to spend millions to upgrade the home team locker room, buy a luxurious new team plane, and book the team into exclusive Ritz Carlton hotels on the road. Pat Riley understands the Armani Principle!

My point is that image and style sells almost any product on this planet! You are a product too. The way you walk, talk, smell, dress, communicate, and radiate success will determine whether you succeed or not. Like it or not, people will judge you and the products you're selling based on how attractive and successful they think you are. Like a car or house for sale, you must appear shiny, new, valuable, special, exclusive, and in demand. That's the image that sells! If you seem unsuccessful or desperate, no one will buy what you are selling. They will assume what you are selling has no value.

Am I exaggerating the importance of image? Judge for yourself. A study of MBA grads found that good looks translated into a higher starting salary for men. For women, the payoff was even more startling. By the end of their first decade on the job, good looks added up to almost ten thousand per year in higher annual salary!

A study of two thousand lawyers found that unattractive lawyers made substantially less money fifteen years after law school. I was listening to a talk radio station in Los Angeles when this study was the topic of discussion. Attorneys called in by the dozens to report that the study was correct—that well-dressed lawyers attract the big clients and win the big cases. In other words, the way an attorney looks determines the guilt or innocence of his or her client! Pretty sad, but true!

Then there are the amazing results of an experiment in the Long Beach, California school system. Long Beach schools were typical of most trouble-plagued urban schools in California—lots of crime, truancy, gangbangers, drug dealers, teen pregnancy, fights, and other bad news. To combat those growing problems, Long Beach became the first major public school system in the nation to institute a mandatory dress code. Criticism and skepticism abounded. How could a dress code change children's behavior? It did—drastically! The results:

- A 36 percent drop in crime
- A 51 percent drop in fights
- A 74 percent drop in sex offenses

- An 80 percent drop in weapons offenses
- A 34 percent drop in battery
- An 18 percent drop in vandalism
- A 33 percent drop in suspensions

A dress code dramatically affected the self-esteem of these children. The way they looked and dressed gave them pride. The way they looked affected the decisions they made on a daily basis. The way they looked gave them more discipline.

The way you choose to dress and look can and will dramatically affect your life as well!

POSITIVE ADDICTIONS

Be an Exercise Addict!

Along with prayer and meditation, exercise—physical fitness—may be your most valuable addiction. I've experimented for years and found three hard and fast rules that apply to exercise:

1. Do it every day—without exception.

2. Do it in the morning when your energy is highest. The kids are asleep, the phones aren't ringing, and you can avoid distractions. If you save it for later, you probably won't do it at all.

3. Do it at home—if you join a gym, you will go for a few weeks or months, but gradually—over time—you'll burn out. In the time it takes most gym-rats to drive to their gym and back, I've already finished my workout.

By working out at home, I've also managed to turn workout time into family time. That's a natural added bonus—the family factor. We all live in a stressed-out, time-deficient world. There's rarely enough quality time for your family. The time you spend at the gym, surrounded by strangers, is the time you could have spent surrounded by the people you love—the people who need your love, support, and presence. By working out at home—in my own personal gym—I've added an hour or two a day to the time I spend with my wife and daughter Dakota.

One more bonus to working out at home: my daughter is learning about a healthy lifestyle at a young and impressionable age. As I write this book, Dakota has just turned four years old. Yet she has been raised around two parents who make exercise a regular and important part of their lives. That's her whole life's experience! So she believes that getting up in the morning and working out with Mom and Dad is how all kids start their day. Studies prove that what we learn as kids will become a pattern for the rest of our lives. If we learn bad habits—a sedentary life, eating junk and fast foods—obesity and illness will become a natural part of our life. If we learn positive lifestyle habits—exercise and healthy living will become a natural part of our life. By working out at home I've hit the lottery: I've extended my life span, reduced my chances of illness, increased my energy, improved the way I look and feel, raised my self-esteem, improved my sex life, produced a healthier heart, given myself confidence that I can reach my goals in life, and spent quality time with my family. I've made it possible for my daughter to extend her life span and reduce her chances of mental or physical illness—all by the age of four! The moral to this story is that the family that works out together, stays together. Now that's my definition of health insurance!

Keep in mind you do not need an expensive, elaborate gym. Health and fitness is my life, my light, and my motivation—so I've chosen to build an elaborate gym. Eventually you may become an exercise addict too. You may want to create a state-of-the-art gym—a room that will be the centerpiece of your home. But in the meantime, I'd simply recommend a treadmill, exercise bike, or cross-country skier set up in front of a television (that's the one time TV is okay—if it gets you through a workout, it has finally served a positive purpose). Eventually you may want to add a second piece of equipment for variety. But for now, one or two aerobic exercise machines will suffice. Don't try to complicate matters—start out by keeping it simple.

> **"A workout is a personal triumph over laziness and procrastination. It is the badge of a winner—the mark of an organized, goal-oriented person who has taken charge of his or her destiny."**
>
> *President's Council on Physical Fitness*

That brings up another issue near and dear to my heart. As I travel the country spreading my exercise and healthy living message, I often encounter the following resistance: "Well, of course it's good for me, and of course exercising at home would be beneficial. But I don't have the money or the time." My answer is "Nonsense." It all comes down to goals and tenacity again. If you agree that you'd like to set up a home gym—find a way to do it. Create a goal, a game plan, and budget.

As far as time is concerned, exercising at home saves you time. And exercising adds years to your life—so you get extra time to do the things you love to do! As far as money, learn to prioritize. I read a study on cigarettes recently. The researchers who conducted the study added up the lifetime costs of smoking—purchase of cigarettes, higher medical bills, higher life and health insurance rates, missed time at work due to illness, and the interest over a lifetime on all those extra bills. The average cost of smoking over a lifetime: $1 million! As the article later put it: "Enough for a mansion on the beach and a Jaguar in the driveway." I guess it isn't a coincidence that I own an estate at the beach with a convertible Jaguar in the driveway! What I'd like to add to that study is the amount of money spent on alcohol, higher medical bills due to alcohol consumption, alcohol rehabilitation fees, higher insurance rates, missed work due to alcoholism and cirrhosis of the liver, and interest on all those bills. I'd guess we're talking another cool million! Now add in drug use and abuse. Get the picture! Millions of Americans abuse drugs, alcohol, and cigarettes. Yet they wonder why they haven't got the money to improve their standard of living? Over the course of a lifetime that kind of self-destructive lifestyle adds up to $2 to $3 million wasted up their nose, into their liver, and up in smoke! If you have the money for cigarettes, alcohol, or drugs, you have the money to work out, raise your self-esteem, and change your life. If you'd stop drinking or smoking for just a few months, you'd save enough to buy a piece of exercise equipment. And if you'd use that equipment religiously every morning for a few months, you'd become more addicted to the sense of accomplishment and self-esteem you'd feel than you ever were to drugs, alcohol, or cigarettes! That new positive feeling would translate to hundreds of thousands—if not millions—of dollars over the course of a lifetime.

> **"If sedentary Americans would change their habits... there would be enormous benefits to the public's health, with significant impact on the cost and delivery of health care."**
>
> *Los Angeles Times*

Now to the "how" part of exercise. I treat exercise as a two-part process: natural and planned. Natural exercise takes advantage of nature. We were not created by God to sit in chairs all day looking at a computer screen, followed by lying in bed all night watching television. Our lifestyles have changed, but not our bodies—our bodies were created to walk everywhere, work with our hands, hunt in the woods, work in the fields, and sleep under the stars. I believe all of us must find ways to put more physical activity into our everyday lives. Here are a few simple ideas for making your daily life more physically and naturally active:

- Walk or bicycle to work instead of driving.

- Take the stairs instead of the elevator at work.

- Bring a workout outfit to the office and skip lunch. Take an hour walk or hike instead. Then snack on small meals throughout the workday.

- Organize outdoor outings with family and friends. Spend your time together hiking, biking, swimming, skating, skiing—instead of sitting on sofas talking, gossiping, playing cards, or watching television.

- Organize business functions and seminars around outdoor, goal-oriented, and team-building events— mountain climbing, rappelling, biking, hiking, camping, kayaking, etc.

- Start a garden—even a little one.

- Use weekends to discover new sports and hobbies designed to get you off the sofa and out of the house.

- Make a connection between "family time" and outdoor activities: Play softball, volleyball, or basketball, hike, bike, swim—all together as a family unit. A family bike ride every Saturday morning is much more beneficial than a family outing to the fast-food restaurant.

- Finally, make nature a part of your life. If you're fortunate to live near beaches, mountains, forests, lakes, and streams—take advantage of them! Even if you live in a big city, you can find parks, public gardens, arboretums. Be creative. Get outside and move!

"Planned exercise" is the alter ego to natural exercise. Just as its name suggests, planned refers to exercise that is planned or created by man—usually indoors, in a controlled and timed setting. There are three areas of benefit to planned exercise:

Number one is aerobic. This is exercise that gets your heart rate and breathing up and keeps them there long enough to have a strengthening effect on your cardiovascular and respiratory systems. Some good examples are running (on a treadmill or outdoors), skiing (cross-country or on a ski machine), rowing (outdoors or on a rowing machine), stair climbing (on real stairs or on a machine), bikeriding (outdoors or on a stationary bike), dancing, or simply a good aerobics class.

Number two is strength training. This is exercise that builds muscle strength and mass. It includes exercise done with weight machines (or free weights) and calisthenics (push-ups, pull-ups, sit-ups, etc.) This kind of exercise has some of the same benefits as aerobic exercise, but it also has benefits all its own—it helps you burn fat more efficiently, decreases the risk of bone loss with aging, improves your appearance, and reduces the risk of injuring underdeveloped muscles. Recent studies prove that the benefits of weight training apply at any age—even eighty- and ninety-year-olds experienced dramatic improvements in heart rate and strength within weeks of undertaking a weight training program!

Number three is flexibility conditioning. This is exercise that increases your range of motion, making it possible for you to use each of your joints fully and effectively. Yoga is the best exercise I have found to increase flexibility. The benefits of flexibility conditioning are improved grace and balance and reduced risk of sports injuries caused by muscle tightness. You can get a book on yoga at any library or bookstore. Or you can take a yoga class in virtually any major city. Learn five to ten basic exercises and then do them at home before or after you exercise. What makes yoga one of my personal favorites is that the mental benefit is equal to or better than the physical benefit—yoga reduces stress and uplifts my spirits!

Ideally, a person should get at least a half-hour of aerobic exercise three to five times a week, a half-hour of strength training two or three times a week, and ten to fifteen minutes of flexibility conditioning two to three times per week. Does that sound like a lot of exercise? All it adds up to is forty to fifty minutes every day of the week. (Hint: That's the commuting time you save by building a home-based business.) You don't have to start off like gangbusters.

> **"Ninety percent of successful dieters exercise regularly, compared with 34 percent of yo-yo dieters."**
>
> *Vogue magazine*

Start with a ten-minute walk every day. Build up to twenty minutes. Then start to add in or substitute other aerobic, strength, and flexibility exercises. Soon you will be addicted. And in a world where addictions usually revolve around cigarettes, coffee, alcohol, recreational drugs, prescription drugs, and junk food, yours is an addiction to be proud of!

AUTHOR'S NOTE: *Be sure to consult your physician before making any significant changes in your physical* *habits (exercise, diet, or nutritional supplementation). Please understand that the recommendations in this book are not intended as a substitute for the regular care of your family doctor or other medical practitioner.*

Be a Healthy Diet Addict!

You'll need energy and enthusiasm to achieve your goals. A healthy diet and lifestyle lead to enormous amounts of energy, vitality, and pure get up 'n' go! Think of your body as a $150,000 Ferrari convertible. An expensive foreign sports car doesn't run on cheap, low-octane fuel. A Ferrari requires special handling and maintenance. It requires some old fashioned TLC—tender, loving care! So do you! Your body is like a delicate racing machine. In addition to getting out on the road frequently—exercise—your body requires special fuel: healthy food. Junk food, fast food, frozen dinners, high-fat food, and foods laced with chemicals, preservatives, pesticides, hormones, and antibiotics will damage and decay your engine. The result will be a lack of energy, enthusiasm, and optimism, a lack of focus and creativity, and eventually—illness and disease.

> **"Eating less fat and taking a brisk... daily walk can—in less than a month—virtually eliminate what researchers have called a 'deadly quartet' of heart disease risk factors."**
>
> *USA Today*

My healthy diet addiction is a simple, practical approach to better eating. I'm not—I repeat not—going to ask you to give up hot dogs, hamburgers, sodas, pizzas, desserts, steaks, pretzels, spaghetti, french fries, pancakes, bacon, and all of those other high-fat, delicious, "bad for you" foods. You won't get any dramatic lectures from me demanding you make extreme changes in your diet. I won't ask you to spend the rest of your life eating salads, carrot sticks, tofu, and bean sprouts. You and I both know that for most people, that's never going to happen. First of all, very few of us can stick to a diet that boring and unappetizing. Second, to eat a diet like that would require willpower very few of us are born with—especially in a society that advertises and promotes junk food everywhere we turn. Finally, that diet would require that you abandon all your friends and business acquaintances—who'd want to spend time with you if all you ate was tofu and bean sprouts?

> **"Tell me what you eat, and I will tell you what you are."**
> *Anthelme Brillat-Savarin*

What I'm asking you to do is to moderate your eating habits. I'm asking for small changes. And instead of tofu, I'm going to introduce you to all the "comfort foods" you were raised eating—updated and made healthy and fat-free for the Nineties! Most of my healthy diet addiction ideas are courtesy of my wife Debra—A.K.A. Mrs. Malibu. Her cookbooks, diet program, cooking videos, and nonfat peanut butter will soon be available in supermarkets and health food stores nationwide. She creates meals that not only taste good, but are nonfat too! None of our family or friends can believe it. Nothing that tastes that good could possibly be nonfat—but of course it is! We'll get to the diet in a moment. But first let's examine the components of your newfound healthy diet addiction:

- **Eat a low-fat diet.** If you only made this one change and nothing else, you would almost certainly lose weight, reduce your risk of heart disease and cancer, and feel healthier and more energetic. The average American gets about 40 percent of his or her daily calories from fat. Most studies recommend about half that amount—around 20-25 percent. So how do you reduce the fat in your diet without sacrificing taste and satisfaction? Here are some suggestions to get you started:

- **Find alternatives to frying** (example: chicken can be baked and still have a crispy crust).

- **Exchange high-fat items** for lower-fat ones that still please you (examples: a fresh whole grain bagel with low-fat cream cheese, instead of a high-fat morning muffin with butter; pretzels instead of chips).

- **Reduce cooking oils and fats** (example: use half the amount of oil called for in a stir-fry recipe and add a bit of chicken broth or water for extra moisture).

- **Find lower-fat versions** of items you enjoy (examples: skim or 1 percent milk; low-fat cheeses and yogurt; soy milk; ground turkey; low-fat or fat-free salad dressings). If you have a sweet tooth, look for lower-fat ways to satisfy it (examples: fat-free cookies; whole grain, honey-sweetened apple pie instead of apple strudel; nonfat frozen yogurt instead of high-fat ice cream).

If you're mathematically minded, you can also apply an easy formula to any packaged foods you buy: Find the number of grams of fat per serving and multiply it by nine (for instance, 3 grams of fat x 9 = 27). Then look at the total number of calories per serving. Your best choices are foods where the fat number per serving is one-third or less of the total (for instance, 27 out of 100 calories per serving).

You'll find that as you eat less fat, you'll start to crave it less. After a few months, rich sauces, premium ice cream, and fried foods will start to taste greasy and unappealing and will feel heavy and indigestible in your stomach. That may be hard to believe, but try it and see!

- **Eat more**: No, not more food—but more often. A number of clinical studies have shown that when animals eat less, they live much longer, maintain youthful vigor and metabolism, and seem better able to ward off age-related diseases. The easiest way to eat less is to eat smaller meals several times throughout the day—that way you are never too hungry and are less likely to pig out on huge quantities of food. You'll feel light, satisfied, and full of energy—you won't experience heartburn, upset stomach, or those middle of the day power outages anymore! Your energy will stay consistently high all day long.

- **Don't be too extreme**: Our eating habits are built up over a whole lifetime. For most of us, tastes, textures, specific foods, and food-connected rituals have deep associations with family, love, comfort, and fulfillment. Changing your eating habits (even when it makes sense and you feel motivated) isn't an overnight thing. I encourage you to make changes at a rate that you can sustain. Look for healthy alternatives that provide a feeling of comfort and satisfy your taste buds. Explore the world of healthy food—don't think you have to renounce pleasure to be healthy! Experiment until you find healthy alternatives that taste great too!

- **Increase your intake of natural, unprocessed foods:** This includes whole grain flours and the products made from them (bread, crackers, pretzels, cereals, pastas); grains (brown rice, millet, barley, oats, dried corn); legumes (beans and peas); vegetables (potatoes, peppers, broccoli, carrots), and whole sweeteners (rice syrup, malt syrup, molasses, sorghum, maple syrup). Unlike simple carbohydrates like white flour and refined sugars, these whole foods are digested slowly, providing steady energy, rather than a quick energy rush (and letdown). Most complex carbohydrates also have lots of fiber, which reduces your risk of cancer, helps your digestion and elimination, and keeps you feeling satisfied longer after you eat. Try to purchase organic products whenever possible.

So it seems I've created a contradiction here. On one hand, I'm telling you that it's possible to eat the comfort foods you've spent your life eating. And on the other hand, I'm telling you to eat healthy, lighter meals. I feel like a Nike commercial starring Deion Sanders—do you eat healthy, low-fat food or heavy, comfort food? How about both! You can literally have your cake and eat it too!

I can't stand veggies. I'm not a fruit fan either. I can't stand tofu or bean sprouts. I despise sprouted bread. I can tolerate brown rice, but just barely! To me, vegetarian food is the pits. Yet I eat a very low-fat, totally healthy, chemical- and pesticide-free diet. I get to eat all my childhood favorite comfort foods—yet now they're good for me. I can eat them knowing that every bite I take is nourishing me and making me healthier, stronger, and even younger! How do I do it? The same way you're now going to do it—with my healthy diet addictions!

• I love hamburgers, cheeseburgers, hot dogs, and fries. Especially on a barbecue! But my alternative is lean turkey burgers or organic beef burgers, with organic goat cheese, on a whole grain bun. My hot dogs of choice are turkey wieners minus the nitrates. My french fries are organic, low-fat potato fries— baked in a convection oven. The buns for my hot dogs and burgers are garnished with healthy, organic ketchup, mayonnaise, and mustard. You can buy these healthy condiments at any health food store. They contain organic ingredients with less salt and sugar and no preservatives, artificial flavorings, or colorings. I might add a pickle on the side—it too is bought in a health food store and produced without chemicals or preservatives.

- I love pancakes, eggs, and sausage for breakfast. But my alternative is whole grain pancakes, pure natural organic syrup, organic egg whites, and organic, low-fat turkey sausage.

- For dessert I love vanilla-frosted cake with vanilla ice cream or vanilla cookies with milk. But my alternatives are whole grain vanilla cake made with whole wheat flour, rice milk, organic eggs, and Florida Crystals® (evaporated cane sugar). My ice cream is organic nonfat yogurt or rice cream (ice cream made from rice), or whole grain, fruit-sweetened, fat-reduced vanilla cookies with low-fat rice or soy milk.

- For a snack, I'll eat pretzels, potato chips, popcorn, or caramel corn—the same snacks you probably eat. But my pretzels are low-fat sourdough or whole grain with sea salt; my potato chips are reduced-fat organic potato slices that were baked, not fried; my popcorn is organic, air popped, with sea salt; and my caramel corn is nonfat, made from organic corn and sweetened with Florida Crystals® (a great alternative to highly processed and nutritionless white sugar. I use it on almost everything!).

- I was raised in New York on pizza and pasta and I still love eating them. Now I can gorge on them without giving myself heartburn! My alternative is a whole grain or rice crust pizza, topped with organic goat cheese, lots of organic onions and garlic, and free-range chicken. My pasta is whole grain, with pure virgin olive oil, and lots of garlic and peppers. A variety of healthy pastas and pizzas are available at any health food store or gourmet supermarket.

- I love breads. I could live on bread, muffins, pastries, bagels, cookies, Danish, French toast, and pancakes. If I had a choice, my last one meal—I'd order a five-course meal of bread, bread, and more bread! Yet the breads I eat are all organic whole wheat or whole grain, low-fat or nonfat, and sweetened with natural sweeteners. I'm not damaging my immune system with every bite—I'm actually strengthening my immune system!

The meals I just described are delicious, healthy, and non- or low-fat. Most actually taste better than the high-fat, high-cholesterol, chemical- and sugar-laced originals. The important point is that innovative alternatives like these make it possible for anyone to eat healthy. Now you can eat what you crave without risking your health or your life (illnesses like heart disease, cancer, strokes, diabetes, ulcers, and obesity are all to some degree diet related). All of these healthy alternatives are available at any local health food store and in many high-quality supermarkets. They cost a little more, but aren't you and your family worth it? In the long run they are inexpensive—they'll save you tens of thousands—perhaps hundreds of thousands—in doctor visits, hospital stays, lowered health insurance rates, and higher rates of productivity at the workplace! Once again, that's my definition of health insurance!

ORDINARY BREAKFAST FOODS:
Frosted cereal with milk and sugar
Coffee with cream and sugar
High-fat muffin with butter
Pancakes with maple-flavored syrup and butter
Eggs fried in butter, bacon, and biscuits

MY HEALTHY ALTERNATIVES:
Whole grain cereal with skim milk (or soy milk), with fresh fruit
Herb tea with honey
Whole grain, nonfat muffin with Neufchâtel or nonfat cream cheese
Wholegrain pancakes and real maple syrup (don't need butter!)
Ranch eggs, cooked in a nonstick pan, low-fat turkey bacon, and a wheat onion bagel

LUNCH/DINNER/SWEET FOODS:
Iceberg lettuce and carrot salad with commercial dressing
Ham sandwich on white bread with mayonnaise
Double cheeseburger (dripping with fat) and french fries
Spaghetti and sausage meatballs
Beef stroganoff with egg noodles
Apple pie and ice cream

Hot fudge, high-fat brownie sundae with whipped cream

MY HEALTHY ALTERNATIVES:

Salad of organic greens and vegetables, low-fat natural dressing

Low-fat turkey ham or turkey bologna on whole grain bread with low-fat, natural mayonnaise

Turkey soy cheeseburger on whole wheat bun with organic potatoes, baked lightly with canola oil

Whole grain pasta with ground turkey meatballs, low-fat marinara

Turkey stroganoff with nonfat sour cream and nonfat noodles

Baked apple with nonfat ice milk

Nonfat healthy brownie sundae with fat-free fudge and nonfat frozen yogurt

Here are a few more healthy alternatives:

HOLIDAY MEAL ALTERNATIVES:

Healthy versions of the traditional meals for Thanksgiving or Christmas:

Naturally raised, free-range turkey

Whole grain stuffing with half the butter

Whole grain, low-fat rolls

Organic mashed potatoes with nonfat gravy

Fresh vegetables, lightly cooked with nonfat or low-fat cheese

Fresh cranberries, lightly sweetened with maple syrup and fruit juice

Organic apple cider, or alcohol-free wine or champagne
Naturally sweetened pumpkin pie with low-fat crust
and whipped cream made from natural evaporated
skim milk

ENTERTAINING ALTERNATIVES:
Healthy party food:
Alcohol- and chemical-free wine, champagne, or beer
Sparkling water and fresh fruit juice punch
Fresh fruits and vegetables with low-fat, yogurt-based
dips or salsa
Whole grain crackers or bread with low-fat cheeses
Organic salad greens with low-fat cheese, poultry, or
seafood
Whole grain pretzels with bread sticks
Fresh shrimp or fish with naturally sweetened cocktail
sauce (no chemical additives)
Low-fat frozen yogurt with naturally sweetened, whole
grain cookies
Whole grain, naturally sweetened, reduced-fat pastries
and cakes
Chicken or fish with fresh vegetable shish kebab
Low-fat corn and potato chips with salsa and low-fat
dips
Whole grain, naturally sweetened, reduced-fat pastries
and cakes

AUTHOR'S NOTE: *Be sure to consult your physician
before making any significant changes in your physical
habits (exercise, diet, or nutritional supplementation).*

*Please understand that the recommendations in this
book are not intended as a substitute for the regular care
of your family doctor or other medical practitioner.*

Be an Energy Addict!

Once again—back to the Ferrari analogy! If your body
is a brand-new Ferrari convertible, your exercise addiction will tune it up, your healthy diet addiction is your
high octane fuel, and now your energy addiction will
turbocharge it! You've now got the
hottest car on the road! Everywhere
you go, passersby and other drivers
will stare at your beautiful set of
wheels. That's what great health and
great energy are all about! Health is
wealth. Vitality, energy, and enthusiasm can bring you better relationships
and a more fulfilling career. They can increase your
productivity and sales performance, even improve your
sex life. It takes a lot of energy to be successful. I credit my energy, enthusiasm, passion, and tenacity to a
healthy diet and lifestyle, vigorous exercise, and nutritional supplementation. I don't believe I'd be the person I am today without the help of vitamins, minerals,
herbs, antioxidants, amino acids, superfood products,
and liquid oxygen supplements.

> **"Vitamins promise to
> continue to unfold as
> one of the great and
> hopeful health
> stories of our day."**
>
> Time *magazine*

I've taken megadose vitamin supplements for over
fifteen years and never suffered a single negative side
effect. Vitamins work—period! Today I look better, feel
younger, work and play harder, and stay healthier than

ever before. I've got more energy than when I was a teenager! I rarely, if ever, get sick. When I do, I'm over it in a day, without missing any work or scheduled meetings. I haven't had a stomach virus in ten years. I've only gotten the flu once in the last fifteen years! I haven't taken a prescription medicine in a decade. I haven't taken an over-the-counter medicine—not even an aspirin—in over fifteen years. I don't get headaches. I don't get heartburn. Never had a cavity! My allergies—I was born with severe allergies to almost everything (trees, grass, dust, animal dander, pollen, wheat, soy, dairy, chocolate, peanuts, shellfish, citrus fruits; you name it)—are now virtually nonexistent. I actually live and sleep in the same room as my dogs without any problems! I can run faster and farther than I did in college. I can bench press and curl more than I did in college. I would guess that I'd have been diagnosed as hyperactive as a child. Today my ability to concentrate is higher than it's ever been. I haven't stayed overnight in a hospital since I was seven years old (tonsillitis). I don't have a family doctor—my family has no reason to see one! My daughter—at the age of four—has had three colds in her life, never had the flu, and never had an ear infection! She has never taken an antibiotic. I believe it's safe to say I'm doing something right!

For years, vitamin and nutritional supplementation was considered controversial by the medical establishment. Not today. Finally, after decades of attacks, the Western medical establishment is waking up to the power and effectiveness of nontraditional and unconventional medicine. Doctors, scientists, and medical researchers are confirming by the thousands the enormous health benefits of vitamins and healthy diet. Antioxidants in particular are drawing rave reviews. Even insurance companies are starting to explore the option of allowing visits to chiropractors, acupuncturists, holistic healers, and homeopaths. It's taken several centuries too long, but Western medicine is finally coming around to a holistic way of thinking! In the past year, I've read or watched hundreds of news reports on the power of vitamins to heal illness, to slow aging, and to prevent disease. Doctors are reporting that a program like mine—relying on a healthy, low-fat diet, vigorous exercise, vitamin supplementation, prayer, meditation, yoga, and goal-planning (dealing with life's problems and designing solutions)—not only can prevent disease and aging, but can actually reverse them! The irony is that ideas like mine aren't revolutionary—they're actually old-fashioned. They've been around for thousands of years. Yet we're only now, as a society, getting around to discovering the vast potential of natural healing.

> **"Antioxidants may one day revolutionize health care."**
> Time *magazine*

There are five critical categories of energy addiction. Let's look at each of these categories:

- **Vitamins**: If we all lived a low-stress life in a pollution-free environment, eating completely natural foods and drinking pure water, we probably wouldn't need vitamin supplements. But modern life being what it is, taking high-quality vitamins is essential to optimum health, high energy, and vitality. Vitamins are essential to our health—they fight the negative effects of stress and pollution and keep our heart, skin, eyes, brain, liver, muscles, and other internal organs working well.

A subgroup of vitamins called **antioxidants** can also retard aging and help prevent cancer and immune system damage. Floating through our bodies are "free radicals"—molecules with unpaired electrons that can interfere with the functioning of our vital organs—leading to disease and premature aging. Studies have shown that antioxidants neutralize free radicals, thereby preventing cellular damage. Powerful and effective vitamin antioxidants are C, E, A, and beta carotene.

Most health food stores carry a variety of vitamin combinations: Some are formulated to fight the effects of stress; some are comprehensive daily multivitamins; some contain a combination of antioxidants; some fill the needs of specific groups such as children, athletes, pregnant women, etc. Look for vitamin supplements that fit your specific needs and are made without sugar, coloring binders, fillers, or preservatives. A promising new development is the recent introduction of spray vitamins and the new applications of vitamin patches. These offer the exciting possibility of taking megavitamins without swallowing a pill!

- **Herbal Nourishers:** Many cultures have used plant life to heal for thousands of years. For instance, the Native Americans used foxglove to treat edema, shortness of breath, and heart palpitations—all symptoms we now associate with heart disease. The active ingredient of the foxglove plant is a form of digitalis—a drug used in treating heart disease! Herbal nourishers can be eaten as foods, used to make teas, or used as seasonings. Some of the most healthful and effective herbs are ginseng (an energy enhancer), astralagus, schizandra, echinacea, milk thistle, goldenseal, and reiki and shiitake mushrooms. These herbs are used to strengthen the immune system and improve the body's ability to defend and heal itself.

  Hundreds of other herbs also have medicinal or tonic properties, and again, your local health food store will have a large assortment. For example, tea made of chamomile flowers has a calming effect; ginger and peppermint settle the stomach; and lobelia can relieve headaches. A bitter herb called Pau D'Arco can be used to make a tea that has a natural antibacterial effect and stimulates the immune system. Green tea has been the favorite drink in the Orient for centuries. It has inspired poetry and philosophy. It has been praised as an elixir of life. Numerous studies have proven it effective against cancer. You can safely replace many over-the-counter medications with herbal alternatives that are less expensive, equally effective, and have no toxic side effects!

- **Superfoods**: Certain foods are especially effective in creating true health. A few of the most powerful of these superfoods and their properties are listed below:

  - **Garlic**—antibiotic, digestive aid, and immune stimulant; may prevent tumor formation, lowers blood pressure and cholesterol.

  - **Aloe vera**—externally: heals wounds, burns, and other skin conditions; internally: heals the entire digestive system.

  - **Wheat/barley grass**—contains the most concentrated and easily assimilated doses of vitamins, minerals, enzymes, and trace elements of any plant grown in soil.

  - **Chlorella/spirulina**—the ocean's version of wheat grass, containing concentrated doses of necessary vitamins, minerals, and amino acids; is a pure source of protein for those on a vegetarian diet.

  - **Yogurt**—nonfat, unprocessed yogurt is an easily digested source of excellent quality protein and supplies the intestines with live acidophilus cultures necessary for good digestion. You can also get the benefits of yogurt by taking acidophilus or bifidus capsules.

  - **Cruciferous vegetables**—(broccoli, cauliflower, brussels sprouts, cabbage, and kale) contain sulforaphane, shown to block tumor formation and thus fight cancer. Studies report that people who eat a diet high in cruciferous vegetables have lower rates of cancer. The good news for veggie haters of the world is that this class of veggies is now available via capsule form.

- **Lecithin**—nourishes and builds nerve, brain, and muscle tissue, breaks down arterial cholesterol deposits, protects cells and cell membranes from oxidation, thus slowing the aging process.

- **Digestive enzymes**—help the body break down foods and absorb their nutrients. Papayas are the most concentrated natural food source of enzymes.

- **Bee products**—bee pollen (be careful if you are allergic to pollen), propolis, and royal jelly (the sole food of the queen bee) are all power-packed with high doses of essential vitamins (including all-important antioxidants), minerals, and enzymes. Bee products can boost your energy, help you fight disease by stimulating your immune system, and even prolong your life span.

- **Minerals**: Scientists have found that our bodies need tiny amounts of certain minerals for optimal functioning. These trace minerals are essential to our energy level and our ability to live long and vigorous lives. A few of the most important are:

- **Germanium**—helps the body take in and use oxygen, improving the body's ability to cleanse itself of toxins and repair tissues.

- **Chromium picolinate**—helps maintain a proper metabolic rate, leading to healthy weight loss through the burning of excess fat.

- **Zinc**—stimulates the immune system, helps heal burns and wounds, and keeps the prostate gland and the sex organs healthy.

- **New and Improved Antioxidant Superstars:** While basic vitamins like C, E, and beta carotene have had this category all to themselves in recent years, a whole new generation of exciting antioxidants has moved to the front of the class. These are the new superstars of the antiaging world:

  - **Grape seed extract**—a unique type of bioflavonoid that works in concert with vitamin C. Helps protect and synthesize vitamin C in the body. One of the main free radical scavengers—potentially up to fifty times more powerful than vitamin C or E!

  - **Glutathione**—another potent antioxidant that helps to prevent damage by free radicals.

  - **Coenzyme Q10**—found in every cell in the body, it is essential in energy production. Also prevents formation of unstable oxygen molecules that cause aging and malignant cells.

- **Quercetin**—another hot antioxidant, this bioflavonoid may play an important role in cancer prevention.

- **Selenium**—a mineral that works hand in hand with glutathione to prevent free radical damage. Also plays an active role in detoxifying the body.

- **Liquid stabilized oxygen**—without a proper supply of oxygen, our bodies cannot properly metabolize and absorb vitamins, minerals, or amino acids. Nor can our bodies properly excrete the toxins we breathe and consume daily. Oxygen supports the immune system's battle against disease and aging. Oxygen is what gives us life—the ability to breathe normally. With asthma, bronchial disorders, and viral infections at record highs, adding oxygen supplements to your diet is a must! Oxygen literally creates energy! Oxygen is effective against bacteria, fungi, and viruses. It aids your body in fighting off invading anaerobic pathogens (you won't get viruses, colds, flu, or infections as often!).

"New studies show that scientists ridiculed by mainstream medicine for touting massive intakes of nutrients like vitamin C and E may have been onto something."

The New York Times

All of the energy-creating and immune-stimulating nutritional supplements included in my energy addiction program can be found at your local health food store. Many occur naturally in a variety of healthy foods. But if like me, you're not a vegetable or fruit fan, or you simply cannot stomach eating entire meals of green superfoods, you're going to have to supplement your diet. In the case of antioxidants, you couldn't possibly eat enough vegetables, fruits, or seaweed to provide you with the antioxidant levels necessary to keep you young, strong, and free of illness and disease—not in a modern world full of air pollution, chlorinated and fluoridated water, pesticide-laced vegetables and fruit, hormone- and antibiotic-laced meat and poultry, and massive amounts of stress facing us every day! If you want to keep your energy high, your stress low, and your attitude positive, you have no choice but to supplement your diet!

> "Almost every week brings new hints that extra doses of vitamins may help you stay healthy longer."
>
> Time *magazine*

My suggestion to each of you is to do some research to find out which supplements might be the most beneficial for your personal and unique needs. Never pop pills indiscriminately. Experiment slowly and carefully. Be aware of food allergies, and by all means, stop taking any supplement that makes you feel bad or causes a negative reaction. Get ready for the energy high of your life!

One more thought in closing: Many of the most effective and advanced nutritional and energy supplements available today are sold via MLM (multi-level marketing) organizations. Research the opportunities available to you. This may be a perfect opportunity to combine your new health addiction with a wealth addiction. There is nothing in this world that warms my heart more than an opportunity to do good for yourself and others, while at the same time building financial freedom for your family. Good luck!

AUTHOR'S NOTE: *Be sure to consult your physician before making any significant changes in your physical habits (exercise, diet, or nutritional supplementation). Please understand that the recommendations in this book are not intended as a substitute for the regular care of your family doctor or other medical practitioner.*

Be an Armani Addict!

I've already explained how important image is (Giorgio Armani is my definition of the "best." His clothes define THRIVER—they are expensive, elegant, and exude success. Hence the name Armani Principle). You are no different than the products on the shelves or racks of your favorite store. The people you meet on a daily basis are shopping. They will look at your "package" and decide if you are exclusive and unique, or plain, boring, and a dime-a-dozen. We can't all be Farrah Fawcett, Cindy Crawford, or Tom Selleck. But anyone can take common sense steps to improve their image. Let's take a look at a few simple Armani Addictions:

- As we've just pointed out, exercise, eat right, and take nutrition supplements. When you are healthy and physically fit, you feel and look more optimistic, confident, and successful.

- Get a stylish new haircut and style.

- Go to a spa or join a diet center and lose that extra twenty pounds. Study after study proves that excess weight will cost you thousands of dollars over the course of your career—for both women and men.

- Get a tan. Aristotle Onassis—one of the world's richest men, once gave his secret to success: "Get up early and always have a tan!" Spend time in the sun—in moderation—and enjoy the feeling of confidence you get from a nice tan. Always wear protective sunscreen and try not to stay out during the hottest and strongest hours of the day. Having a moderate tan is a necessary part of a successful image. A tan makes you look healthy, rested, and successful—the subconscious message being conveyed is that only an individual of substance—living a life of leisure—could manage a perpetual tan! That's an image you'll need to perpetuate on the road to success.

> **"You've got to first look and feel like a million dollars, before you can make a million dollars."**
>
> *Wayne Allyn Root*

- Upgrade your wardrobe. All it takes is a little education and attention to detail. Read magazines like *GQ, Esquire, Vanity Fair, Vogue*, and *Cosmopolitan* each month. Find out what styles and designers are "in." Then buy clothes that project an image of style and success. Remember—like it or not—others will judge you by the image you project. Make that first impression a positive one! As far as the expense of buying designer clothes—do your homework. Shop around for the best prices, negotiate (even the most exclusive boutiques will negotiate to close a sale), and buy at sales, closeouts, and clearance events. But in the end, remember that elegant clothing isn't a purchase—it's an investment in your future success!

- Upgrade the tools of your trade. Invest in a car that projects success, an elegant watch or jewelry, a stylish briefcase, an office that spells power, business cards and brochures that present a successful image. No successful salesperson or businessperson can thrive without a cellular phone, personal computer, laptop computer, fax, and e-mail. Those are just basics at this point. You must be willing to invest in these tools of the trade or you will be left behind.

- Project a more confident image by standing up straight, shaking hands firmly, and looking others directly in the eyes.

- Finally, a more controversial suggestion: Some of you may want to invest in plastic surgery. Many of us have suffered from low self-esteem our whole lives because of a small imperfection or a nagging problem. By fixing that problem, it's possible to turn around your life. You can turn that low self-esteem into confidence. That confidence can translate into better relationships, a better career, a more fulfilling life! So plastic surgery is also an investment in a better you! It's not for everyone, but it may be a possible solution to your unique personal situation.

As far as how you'll afford these investments in your image, my answer is simple—prioritize. Stop watching television and start a second job or career. Stop wasting your money on cigarettes, drugs, and alcohol. Cut down on your food bill. Stop eating out. Do whatever you have to do to upgrade your image. Your future earnings potential will depend on it! Congratulations! You are now an Armani Addict!

Step 4: Do It Boldly!

POWER PRINCIPLES

The New York Principle

This principle goes hand in hand with thinking big. Dreaming up your goal is only half the battle. Now you've got to fight for what you want! The New York Principle is what New Yorkers call chutzpah. Yes, New Yorkers are pushy and aggressive. Yes, New Yorkers are sometimes a little too confident—they often cross the line toward cocky. Yes, they do bother people until they get what they want! Yes, that attitude can get on your nerves. But whether you like it or not, that attitude is integral to success. Quiet, shy, unassuming, polite people do not get what they want out of life. Keep in mind, I'm not telling you to hurt others. I'm not telling you to take advantage of others. I am telling you that one of the realities of life is that if you don't ask, you don't get! The world is full of all kinds of people, with all kinds of goals. You will not be heard unless you speak up! You must tell people what's on your mind. You must pursue your dreams with tenacity and aggressiveness. You must sometimes shout to be heard. You must speak up or you will be forgotten. You must believe in yourself or no one else will. These are all attributes of New York Attitude.

> **"Keep on asking and you will keep on getting; keep on looking and you will keep on finding; knock and the door will be opened."**
>
> *Luke 11:9*

Anyone can learn New York Attitude. My proudest success story is my wife Debra. She is my boldest experiment in human psychology. Debra is by nature everything our model New Yorker is not: loving, kind, sensitive, patient, compassionate, and always polite. Born in the Midwest, a former Miss Oklahoma, she learned early to always think of others first.

What she didn't learn was how to think big and aim high. She didn't learn how to set goals and take action. She didn't learn how to go after what she wanted and get it. How to fight, kick, claw, and scream in order to turn her dreams into a reality. How to shout in order to be heard. How to set herself apart from the crowd. Those are all ideas that did not come naturally. But of course—I changed all that!

Today, Debra is my star pupil. She graduated my mini-boot camp with honors. She is now classified by the Department of Defense as a lethal weapon. She managed to retain all her charm, her compassion, and her loving nature. She managed to retain her spirituality—her devotion to God is still number one. Yet she added confidence, aggressiveness, mental toughness, and a strong dose of chutzpah. Debra is now unstoppable. She is fearless. She goes after what she wants and she gets it! She recently invented nonfat peanut butter that tastes great! Then she added nonfat cheese-

> **"The squeaky wheel gets the grease."**
>
> *Ancient Proverb*

cake, nonfat chocolate mousse, nonfat vanilla cake, nonfat maple cake, nonfat tiramisu, and nonfat lasagna. And they all taste better than the real thing! Then she created her own company—Mrs. Malibu. That's right—my wife is Mrs. Malibu! She's a whirlwind. She wined and dined investors. She raised money, found manufacturers and distributors. She designed logos and labels. And Mrs. Malibu's products are about to hit gourmet supermarkets and natural food stores nationwide!

I've created a monster. Debra puts me to shame. She is a dynamo. She has learned how to utilize action, passion, energy, enthusiasm, and tenacity. You can too!

The New York Principle has been used by all sorts of successful superachievers since the beginning of time. Christopher Columbus utilized it to raise funds for his voyages to the New World in 1492! He traveled Europe to meet with kings and queens to raise his funds. Not only did he ask loudly, forceful, and often, he asked for a lot! His requests were shocking—he demanded a share of any goods he transported, the governorship of any lands he discovered, the title of admiral, a noble rank, a flotilla of ships, and an army of men. These requests were unheard of. No other explorer had ever before dreamed of asking for so much. Christopher Columbus had big dreams, a lot of confidence, and a lot of nerve. Yes, he was rejected by most every king in Europe—several times. But eventually he heard a *yes*. All you need is one *yes* in life! But you've got to dream big, plan big, and ask big to get that one *yes*! Columbus will never be forgotten—his place in history is assured because of his big, bad, bold New York attitude!

In more modern times there's Lee Iacocca. Iacocca took over the presidency of a failing company—Chrysler Corporation. The same day Chrysler hired Iacocca, they announced the worst deficit in their history! Things only got worse from that point. By 1979, the world economy was collapsing, gas prices were doubling, and Chrysler was failing. Iacocca decided to ask for the impossible—only a man with New York attitude would even think of going to the United States government for a loan! Politicians laughed. His competitors complained. Critics were enraged: they screamed "corporate welfare." They complained that the government should not play favorites with one company. They pointed to the free enterprise system and the thousands of companies that had failed throughout history. Most of all they pointed to the circumstances of the time: our own government was hurting, businesses were closing by the thousands, workers laid off from sea to shining sea.

Why help Iacocca? Because he had the confidence, nerve, and audacity to ask! He made his case in front of the United States Congress—pointing out that the government was better off guaranteeing loans now, than spending billions more later in welfare and unemployment insurance. It was a bold presentation, and Iacocca caught the imagination of our country. He stood before the American government and he got them to blink first! In just a few years, Chrysler announced the largest operating profit in its history. Iacocca decided to pay back the government loan seven years ahead of schedule! Lee Iacocca became an American hero—the words the media used to describe him were bold, gutsy, daring, imaginative. What they should have said was: "Classic New York attitude."

> **"All things being equal, whoever screams the loudest and longest, pushes the hardest, and demands the most gets the most, succeeds."**
>
> *Wayne Allyn Root*

The New York Principle will be integral for your success, especially if you sell for a living (in one way or another, don't we all?). You will face concrete walls and glass ceilings. You will be told to wait your turn. You will be rejected without being given a fighting chance. You will be ignored. Your path will be blocked by pushy secretaries or assistants who won't even let you in the door. Your job is to be pushier than they. Your job is to shout loud enough to be heard. Your job is to smash through that glass ceiling with a jackhammer or a blowtorch! You have a goal. You must be heard. You must have passion. You must surmount the obstacles. You must bother your target again and again—until he or she is so tired of you, that they'll see you and hear your pitch—just to get you off their back! Like it or not, that's how you achieve success in the real world.

By the way, a recent survey by the Lutheran Brotherhood reported that only 22 percent of all adults asked for a raise at their job last year! Of that small group, more than half got their raise. I repeat—if you don't ask, you don't get. Start dreaming big and start asking big!

The Tenacity Principle

When I think of tenacity, I think of the story of a resistance fighter in a country occupied by enemy troops. All his compatriots huddle in fear in their homes. But this brave man stands all day and night digging a ditch while repeating "23, 23, 23, 23."

The enemy soldiers assume he's crazy. They ignore him for days. But this monotonous "23, 23, 23, 23" chanting is driving them crazy. Finally, one officer can't take it anymore—he walks over to the crazy man and confronts him.

"Hey, you! Why are you repeating 'twenty-three' all the time?"

"Look in the hole," says our fighter.

The officer looks down into the ditch. Our resistance fighter lifts up his shovel and smashes him in the head. Clang!

The officer falls unconscious into the hole.

As the brave fighter buries him alive, he begins chanting "24, 24, 24, 24."

That's tenacity—a single-minded determination to succeed! Some may call it obsession, others tunnel vision. What it is, is an almost fanatical determination to reach a goal, to achieve, to thrive! That's the attitude you need to overcome failure—you may need to move forward one small step at a time. You may win the war by winning one small battle at a time. You may finish the marathon by reaching one telephone pole at a time. But in the end, all that matters is that you have achieved your goal. Nobody asks you how you did it. No one cares how long it took or what you sacrificed. They only care for the results. If you're the winner at the finish line, you are a THRIVER!

Based on the following examples it seems the female gender may have a lock on the principle of tenacity.

Tammy Bruce, former president of the Los Angeles Chapter of N.O.W. (National Organization for Women) and one of the top radio talk shows hosts in Los Angeles, utilized tenacity to single-handedly derail O. J. Simpson and change the rules of conduct of news organizations around the world! When O. J. was first acquitted, I assumed he'd make tens of millions of dollars off of book deals, television tabloid interviews, pay-per-view specials, and the sale of his video via infomercial. But Tammy Bruce—one lone voice—decided she could single-handedly change the world. She organized a nationwide protest and threatened a coast-to-coast boycott of any media organization, television network, publisher, or promoter who coddled O. J. and enabled him to profit off the deaths of Nicole Brown and Ronald Goldman. Tammy Bruce shamed profit-hungry media and entertainment conglomerates into shunning O. J.—for fear of losing ratings and millions of dollars to angry viewers nationwide. Overnight, all of O. J.'s deals and opportunities evaporated. No major company would touch him. One woman made a difference. One woman stood up to O. J. Simpson. One woman changed the way billion-dollar companies do business. Great job, Tammy Bruce—I applaud your tenacity!

Elaina Valdez also utilized tenacity to change the world against insurmountable odds. Her son Tony was misdiagnosed and rendered sterile by a doctor. She tried to sue for malpractice, but under Florida law the time required to sue had passed. Instead of giving up or complaining, Valdez decided to fight the bureaucracy and change the law. She took on the two most powerful lobbies in the state all by herself—the insurance industry and doctors. She lobbied nonstop—day and night—via phone, fax, and countless trips to the state capitol. Despite setback after setback, she kept fighting. Finally in May 1996, Valdez, a mother and waitress, beat the insurance and medical lobbies! "Tony's Bill" was signed into law by the governor of Florida! Elaina Valdez proves one person with tenacity can change the world!

But in the end, there is only one story that literally defines tenacity. It's a story very close to my heart. It's the story of my mother—a woman whose last hours of life proved that tenacity can move mountains. When people ask where I get my tenacity, determination, and commitment from, I need look no further than one of the strongest-willed individuals to ever walk the face of the earth—-Stella Root. When I hear people calling rock stars, dysfunctional actors, and spoiled athletes "role models," I tell them the story of Stella Root—the way my mother handled death was the true definition of a "role model"!

My mother was tenacious all her life. She always got her way. She could outlast anyone! She even handled death with tenacity. She fought breast cancer valiantly for six long years. On four occasions she came back from death's door to make a full recovery. But even she couldn't hold off cancer forever. By April 1992, she was in a coma—surviving only on life support. One night I got the call I hoped against hope would never come— my mother was brain dead. There were no signs of brain activity and her doctors were disconnecting her life support. "Don't rush home to New York," my mother's doctor said on the phone to me. "She'll be dead within the hour—probably within minutes."

But my sister Lori knew better. She told me to hop on "the red-eye" from Los Angeles and she'd tell our mother "to hold on and wait for Wayne." I threw a few clothes in my bag and raced to the airport. My sister held my mother's hand through the night and told her, "Hold on—Wayne's on the way. Just hold on a few more hours. You've got to stay alive until he gets here."

After an hour's drive to the airport, a two-hour wait for my plane, a six-hour cross-country flight and almost two hours taxiing, deplaning, waiting for luggage, and taking a taxi to Westchester County Medical Center in Valhalla—I arrived at my mother's bedside, eleven hours later. I hadn't even stopped at a pay phone to check in. I didn't know what to expect, but I wasn't surprised to see that her heart was still beating! My mother had willed herself to stay alive for over eleven hours. Doctors—"medical experts"— declared her brain dead, yet she survived through the night waiting for me to arrive. I grabbed her hand, told her I loved her, and told her I appreciated what she had done for me, but now it was time to let go. I knew her emaciated body was tired and it was finally time to stop working. I told her it was okay to go—a better place awaited her. Within five minutes of my arrival, her heart monitor started to slow: "Beep.....beep..........beep...............beep................." Flat line. She had hung on for eleven improbable, impossible hours—against all odds. If she was brain dead, how did she know I was on my way? How did she know I'd arrived? Her tenacity had pulled off what I can only describe as a miracle. Tenacity has nothing to do with your brain. It's all about HEART! I'll remember the last sounds of my mother's heart monitor for the rest of my life.

Tenacity and heart kept my mother alive through that long night. What could it do for you? If she could survive without any brain activity—despite doctor's assurances that it was medically impossible—what could you accomplish with tenacity? Could you change your world? Could you make the impossible possible? Could you accomplish what no one before you has ever done? It may not be in your genes. It may not be in your brain. It may not be in your vocabulary. But believe me—it's possible—if it's in your HEART!

The Irons in the Fire Principle

When you study my story, you'll see that I was always a man in perpetual motion. I never stood still long enough to accept defeat. I was too busy working on twenty deals at the same time. If one failed, there were always nineteen more waiting in the wings! That's always been my guiding philosophy—throw enough irons in the fire and you're guaranteed that at least one will work! If not, there's always lots of backup. With backup comes hope. My career is similar to the Olympic flame—eternally burning. But if you let that flame burn out, then all bets are off. Without a flame, there is no hope. And there is no certainty you can ever get that flame restarted. Once your career grinds to a halt, you may never get it back in gear.

Most people settle for a life of mediocrity because they settle for one small flame—one job, one career, one dream. If that flame goes out, they are in oblivion. They have nothing to fall back on. They are unprepared and ill at ease, trying to reignite that flame. They are depressed and tired and unable to think creatively under pressure. They don't have the energy, drive, or confidence to start all over again.

But the people I've met who I'd define as THRIVERS are never satisfied with just one job, one career, or one dream. They are always working on twenty deals at once. They crave action. They like phones ringing, faxes spewing out paper, computers spitting out e-mail all day long, important meetings at all hours of day and night. They always have backup—no one deal means that much to them. No one failure or rejection will ruin their life. THRIVERS understand there is comfort, safety, and security in numbers—the more irons in the fire, the better the chance to create opportunity. To the survivors of the world, this is madness—too much activity, too much stress, too much pressure. To THRIVERS it is security—they understand that it is the only way to guarantee that you will be in control of your life for the rest of your life.

Action isn't pressure. Making too many deals isn't pressure. Having too many meetings isn't pressure. Getting too many offers isn't pressure. Pressure is sitting alone in your house in silence, waiting for the phone to ring. Pressure is standing in the unemployment line. Pressure is sitting by the mailbox the first of the month, waiting for your government check. Pressure is going on job interviews, praying that someone will save your life by giving you a job you despise and a paycheck that barely puts food on your table. Pressure is not knowing how you'll pay the rent this month.

If you choose to live the life of your dreams and to give your family a prosperous future, you have no choice but to live your life by the Irons in the Fire Principle! What are you waiting for? Get cracking!

The Obsession Principle

If passion is integral to success, what is it that gives you an intense level of passion? Energy is only half of the equation. Purpose is the other half. You've got to love what you do! Superachievers are obsessed by their pursuits. They love what they do. That's what triggers passion—how could you be passionate about something you don't enjoy doing? How could you be passionate about something you weren't born to do?

George Burns once said, "The main thing is to get a job and love what you do. That keeps you young. I was old at twenty-seven because I wasn't working. Now I'm young." George was in his late nineties when he made that statement!

People who love what they are doing automatically do it well. I'm not just talking about famous superachievers. I'm really talking about people like Richard Kelly and Bill "Mojo" Lackey—average people, performing average jobs. Richard Kelly was a supermarket grocery sacker for thirty-five years. But he is living proof that passion, enthusiasm, and purpose lead to extraordinary success. He proves that special people stand out in any job. He proves that treating your job—any job—like an obsession, pays off big-time.

What did Kelly do so that's special? How could a grocery sacker stand out? Kelly found a way—he treated customers with respect. He worked hard. He bent over backward to make customers feel special. No request was too small or too much trouble. Often he ran errands or did favors for customers without expecting anything in return—anything to make people happy!

Upon his retirement, Richard Kelly's story made it into the pages of national newspapers! A supermarket grocery sacker from Chicago did his job so well that he was honored thousands of miles away! The articles quoted customers as being heartbroken upon hearing of his retirement. Many customers in the supermarket's upscale neighborhood said they thought of Kelly as a role model for their children! Rival supermarkets tried to steal Kelly away many times over the years. Can you imagine this scenario? Headhunters try to steal six-figure executives. Law firms raid attorneys from rival law firms. But a grocery sacker in demand? Kelly retired as a legend in the supermarket business. He made his mark on the world as a grocery sacker! He also retired with six rental properties and a landscaping business! Special people find a way to stand out in any job, any career, any business.

Bill "Mojo" Lackey wasn't rich or famous either. He also worked at a job you might consider average. But like Richard Kelly, he found a way to make his mark on the world. Lackey died recently of a heart attack. He was equipment manager for the Houston Oilers football team. That's a pretty unremarkable job—he was paid by the hour to wash dirty uniforms and jockstraps. His life was anything but glamorous. He was overweight, had no wife or kids, no assets, didn't even own a suit. He spent most of his adult life in a smelly, sweaty locker room.

Yet upon Mojo's death, macho football players cried like babies. Over a thousand people attended his funeral—many traveled from hundreds of miles away. The Oilers dedicated their next game to him and won. His image on the stadium big screen before the game attracted a standing ovation! Why? What did this simple man do that inspired such adulation? Mojo simply loved his job. He gave 110 percent every moment of every day. For sixteen years he was there to comfort players with a smile, a hug, and a few words of support. He was there to cry with players after an injury. He was there to say "I love you" to retiring players. He was there to give words of encouragement to coaches after a loss. He became so popular with fans, he was asked by kids to sign autographs—he felt so honored, he'd stay for hours after games talking to those children. Mojo loved his job and the whole world loved him! He was more popular than some million-dollar athletes!

So you see, you must find something you love to do and then do it well—do it with passion and enthusiasm! That's all the world asks. Do that and do it well and the world is yours—whether you're a million-dollar-a-year investment banker or a five-dollar-an-hour grocery sacker!

The Promotion Principle

This is another of my powerful real world principles. In an ideal world, we could all sell a great product without having to promote it. The whole world would find us, and we'd sell a gazillion dollars worth of product and change the world. Unfortunately, this isn't an ideal world. In the world we all live in today, we face a crowded and competitive environment. Just having a great product isn't enough. You have to find a way to market yourself or your product that sets you apart from the crowd.

Subzero Freezer did it. A refrigerator is like a microwave or a blender—practical, not sexy, right? Wrong! Subzero found a way to separate itself from the crowd and create a sexy image for a refrigerator. They marketed themselves as "the refrigerator to the stars in Hollywood." They gave away free Subzeros to celebrities. Soon upscale consumers across America had to have one! Instead of charging five hundred dollars for a typical refrigerator, Subzeros sell for $3,500 and up. Sales are growing twice as fast as the refrigerator market as a whole! Sales now total over $135 million per year—proving once again that image sells in the real world.

José Eber did the same thing in the hair business. Barbers all over American eke out a modest living, charging five to ten dollars for a haircut, perhaps even twenty or thirty dollars for a style. But José Eber marketed himself as "the hairstylist to the stars." His star-studded, celebrity clientele attracted thousands of clients willing to pay two hundred dollars and up for a hairstyle! That made José Eber the most famous hair-stylist in America! José Eber found a way to stand apart from the crowd.

Ben & Jerry's Ice Cream did it too. They aren't just a company, they're an experience! Two hundred and fifty thousand people a year visit Ben & Jerry's ice cream plant, making it the most popular tourist destination in Vermont! The annual stockholders' meeting isn't business, as much as two days of gorging on ice cream named after hip celebrities and listening to rock concerts! And then there's the CEO essay contest. That's right, Ben & Jerry's conducted a nationwide search for a new CEO by holding an essay contest—winner take all! It's promotions like that, that have catapulted Ben & Jerry's into the best-selling super premium ice cream in America! The ice cream is delicious, but it's the wild promotions that bring in the customers!

Charities need to find ways to set themselves apart from the crowd too. An order of Roman Catholic priests recently produced a movie called *The Spitfire Grill*. The movie has received critical acclaim, won film festival awards, and most importantly, produced a $4 million profit which will help support programs for the poor. Who says churches need to be socially-minded, but not profit-minded?

Stephen Hilbert found a creative way to promote and finance his insurance company! He couldn't convince a single investment bank to invest in his company. So he took his idea to the people. He decided to sell shares in his company the same way he sold life insurance—door to door. Hilbert and his salespersons knocked on thousands of doors and sold shares worth $4 million to two thousand people in ninety-two counties of Indiana.

Today that company is called Conseco. It is a billion dollar company! Stephen C. Hilbert was the second-highest-paid CEO in America over the past five years—his compensation over that period totaled $232 million dollars!

Anita Roddick is a natural born promoter. This British dynamo called her first hair and skin care shop, The Body Shop. She almost never got out of the starting blocks! Two nearby funeral homes threatened to sue her unless she changed her store's name. But rather than change her name or close shop, Roddick decided to fight back with self-promotion: She contacted the press with a story of powerful businessmen trying to intimidate a defenseless woman, new to the business world. The publicity she got turned into the jump-start she needed for her new business. Today The Body Shop includes 1,400 stores in 46 countries, 2,500 employees and over $750 million in annual revenues!

Steve Wynn found a way to set himself apart from the crowds of casinos in America. He introduced gamblers to nature—a unique combination to say the least! The Mirage Resort and Casino in Las Vegas features dolphins, Bengal tigers, volcanoes, and rain forests for the gambling public. Only a promotional genius like Steve Wynn would have thought to put the drama of nature on stage against beautiful showgirls, craps tables, and lounge lizards. The result is that Mirage Resorts is among the best-run and most profitable corporations in all of American business, and Wynn is single-handedly responsible for turning Las Vegas from a gambling "sin city" into an entertainment and family resort destination!

Promotional ability set Jimmy Buffett apart from the crowd, too. Back in the late 1980s Buffett's career was "wasting away in Margaritaville." Then he convinced Corona Beer to sponsor his concerts. "The Margaritaville Lifestyle" was born. Today there's a Margaritaville store, catalog, newsletter, nightclub, restaurant, and record label. His latest album sold over 1.5 million copies. Buffett now sells over $50 million a year worth of CDs, books, T-shirts, concert tickets, and food. Like Ben & Jerry's, Jimmy Buffett succeeded with promotion. His sales figures rival music legends like The Rolling Stones, Frank Sinatra, and Garth Brooks. Buffett is now on *Forbes* magazine's list of the highest paid entertainers in the world—all because of the unique promotion of one memorable song!

Promotion even works in the sports world. Andre Agassi, Shaquille O'Neal, Michael Jordan, and Troy Aikman—all are famous for being great athletes. They are superstars because of their remarkable talents and achievements. But the Jensen brothers are losers who have parlayed self-promotion into a multimillion dollar payoff! These two flamboyant brothers haven't won a tournament in two years! They're not even ranked in the top twenty in doubles! They often lose in the opening round of doubles tournaments. But for the Jensens, tennis isn't about winning. It's about entertainment and marketing. They ride onto the court on Harley-Davidson motorcycles! They scream and yell and chest-butt each other on the court. They play in a rock band and wear tattoos and long hair. The results: screaming crowds, overflow autograph sessions, more media requests than anyone in all of tennis (except Agassi), their own world-wide web site—with six thousand requests a month, a huge worldwide fan club, the longest sponsor list in ten-nis history, and multimillion dollar annual incomes. They prove that—unfortunately—it isn't the quality of the product that matters anymore: it's your ability to set yourself apart from the crowd.

When it comes to self-promotion, Brian "The Boz" Bosworth puts even the Jensen brothers to shame! Brian was one of the all-time great self-promoters in the history of college athletics! As an All-American for Barry Switzer's Oklahoma Sooners, Brian set his sights on fame and fortune. He attracted controversy and media scrutiny again and again throughout his col-lege career—with his bad-boy swagger, wild antics, and bold statements. By the time he left Oklahoma, "The Boz" was more than a household word—he was a national obsession! Due to injuries, his NFL career was cut short after only three seasons. "The Boz" never made a mark in the NFL—but he made his mark in Hollywood! Bosworth was so successful at parlaying his brash, high-profile image into celebrity, that today he is an action movie star, enjoying million-dollar pay-days on the silver screen! He lives out his movie star life in beautiful Malibu, California, married to his high school sweetheart, and is the father of two beautiful daughters. (Brian is a good friend and neighbor of mine.) "The Boz" may be the only player in the history of football to turn a short, injury-filled, three-year NFL career into Hollywood fame and fortune. He did it with a keen understanding of promotion!

Promotions set these remarkable individuals apart from the crowd in an age where image (unfortunately) is everything. What could you do to set yourself or your product apart from the crowd?

The Change Principle

You can't survive long term in business unless you understand the principle of change. Change is a lot like failure—it is a natural part of life. Those who adapt to change, thrive. Those who don't, fall by the wayside. Let's look at a few great examples of change:

- Television executives understand change. Viewers were tuning out the three major networks in droves. So last year they broke with tradition and dropped commercials between popular prime-time shows. With no time to channel surf between shows, viewers stay glued to the dial. That translates to higher ratings and millions of extra dollars in advertising revenues. Major television programmers understand that change is nothing more than smart marketing.

- Entertainers understand change. Tony Bennett's career was considered dead by the mid '70s. He made his living singing in Vegas lounges. But his son Dan took over the management of Tony's career in 1979. Dan designed a career change—he would reinvent

Tony to the MTV generation. Dan booked his father into college and jazz clubs, rather than casino lounges. Tony produced an MTV video. He licensed his likeness to the hip Fox hit show *The Simpsons*. Tony Bennett is hip and hot again—to a whole new generation! He sold 450,000 albums off his MTV video. For Tony, change was just another word for smart marketing.

- Even restaurants understand change. Juniors Restaurant and Deli in Westwood, California, is a Los Angeles institution. *The Wall Street Journal* ranked Juniors in the top one hundred highest-grossing restaurants in America. This family-run Jewish deli has been around for five decades. But even a successful small business must react to change. David Saul, the second-generation managing partner, reacted to the changing demographic of his customer base. He noticed his customers aging and dying off. Yet he couldn't attract a new generation of younger, healthier customers without a menu change. Today, David has expanded and revamped the Juniors menu to reflect the changes in the dietary habits of a younger generation. Juniors features low-fat, fat-free, and healthy choices in addition to traditional deli favorites. For Juniors, change is nothing more than smart marketing.

Change is nothing more than updating your marketing and promotions for a new generation. If you don't change in reaction to a changing world, the world will leave you behind.

The Patience Principle

While those precious moments of opportunity will eventually come, they may take a while. They may take a lot longer than you'd like. I know they always took much longer than I wanted. As a matter of fact, they seemed to take forever. To a classic Type A like me, every hour of my journey seemed like a day; each day seemed like a week; each week like a month; each month like a year. My dream seemed to take forever. In reality, I achieved dramatic amounts of success in an incredibly short period of time. Dreams are like that! When you're living them, they seem to take forever.

To achieve happiness and peace of mind, you'll need to learn the Patience Principle. Believe me, if I can learn at least a small degree of patience, anyone can.

POSITIVE ADDICTIONS

Be a New York Attitude Addict!

Yes, I've heard it all before—New Yorkers can be rude, loud, obnoxious, and arrogant. They can be insensitive and selfish. Far too often they are perceived as unfriendly to strangers. But I'm not asking you to adopt any of these negative traits. New Yorkers are definitely a little rough around the edges. But scratch the surface and you might find a diamond underneath. You see, New Yorkers also possess some remarkable traits—traits, habits, and attitudes you will need to learn to achieve success in the world. New Yorkers are street fighters. They have learned the hard way to survive and even thrive in the face of difficult odds. They are masters at getting ahead in a rough and tumble business world. No matter how difficult a challenge they face, New Yorkers often find a way to go over it, under it, around it, or smash through it. They face what others would call insurmountable obstacles on an almost daily basis and surmount them! If success in life boils down to your ability to turn lemons into lemonade, New Yorkers are your role models.

Like New Yorkers, you too will face failure, rejection, challenge, pain, disappointment, and even tragedy. I believe you will find it absolutely integral to your future success to adopt their way of thinking—I call it "New York Attitude." The positive attributes New Yorkers bring to the table include discipline, aggressiveness, tenacity, boldness, courage, confidence, high energy, passion, and motivation. New Yorkers are fighters: They know to achieve success—you've got to move mountains. And to move mountains, you cannot accept *no* for an answer!

Here are a few simple ideas that will empower you to start thinking like a New Yorker: Think of things you've been afraid to do your whole life and do them! Approach people you've been afraid to approach. Go after jobs you've passed up in order to play it safe. Go get that advanced degree you've been too busy or too afraid to get. Start that business you've been afraid of starting. If you're afraid of flying, get on an airplane. If you've been afraid of swimming your whole life, take swimming lessons. If there's a certain someone you like, ask them out. If there's a career you've secretly dreamed of, create a game plan to make it happen! Stop wasting your life—decide to go after what you want. Do it quickly, without delay. Do it decisively. Do it boldly! When opportunity knocks—seize it! That's how you turn dreams into reality!

In the past, have you accepted the word *no* without a fight? The next time you are rejected, instead of giving up and quietly accepting defeat, think of an immediate way to turn that *no* into *yes*. Propose your idea on the spot. Tell the individual(s) you are meeting that you never accept a *no* as final and that you always look for a way to compromise—a way to turn every situation into a win for all involved. Now instead of creating an adversary, you've enlisted this other person into your cause—they are now thinking of ways to turn this situation into a positive! If possible, schedule another meeting or series of meetings to discuss additional proposals. Do anything you must to keep the dialogue flowing and lines of communication open. That's how you turn a *no* into a *yes!*

No longer accept *no* for an answer! When you hear a final *no* from a client, potential employer, bank loan officer, your parents, your boss, a member of the opposite sex, etc., immediately find a quiet place and write down a list of one hundred others who could potentially say *yes* to you. Now go out and find them. One simple *yes* erases all the feelings of depression, worry, doubt, fear, rejection, poor self-image, and inadequacy. Never give up—keep making new lists if you have to. Search from one end of the earth to the other. But whatever you do, do not ever give up. Never accept defeat! Do not rest until you hear your *yes*.

Start to look at life as one big "lemons to lemonade" experience. Read all the newspapers, magazines, and books you can get your hands on. As you read stories and biographies of great men and women, stop and think of how their stories apply to your life. Study the obstacles they faced or face today, and think of how you'd overcome those same obstacles. Take notes and categorize them under different types of challenges. Refer back to these notes whenever you're facing obstacles or challenges to your life and see how Lincoln, Grant, Patton, Churchill, FDR, or JFK reacted to their personal crises and moments of doubt. History repeats itself again and again. Prepare yourself to overcome challenges and stand tall—just as other great leaders have done before you.

First, start to expect the best and believe that you deserve the best. Next, ask for the best. Remember, if you don't ask, you don't get! Your boss, your clients, your business associates do not read minds—breathe deep, visualize what you want, affirm it, now prepare a positive presentation and ask for it! If you do this on a regular basis, you will start to receive and achieve things you never dreamed possible!

Learn to always take action. The key to taking action is be willing to risk. New Yorkers are natural risk takers. Everytime they step out the door they are automatically risking! A walk on the street at night is a risk. A jog in Central Park is a risk. Driving is a risk—

you face bad weather, potholes, suicidal cabdrivers, and buses. New Yorkers—just by living—get used to taking risks. So can you. Start to take calculated rational risks: skydive (with a parachute and a certified instructor, of course!), bungee jump, mountain climb, ski, take an auto racing course, run a marathon. Start to conquer your fear of risk and fear of the unknown. The courage and confidence you gain will enable you to start taking the most important risk in life—facing failure and rejection.

New Yorkers don't fold under pressure. They crave stress and pressure. Stress wakes them up, empowers them, enlivens them, keeps them at the top of their game. How can you learn to thrive in the face of stress?

Learn to think creatively and quietly under pressure by reading, working, playing chess or backgammon, doing crossword puzzles, etc.— all with a stereo blasting nearby at its highest levels. At first it will be distracting. You will find yourself unable to concentrate. But keep practicing ten to twenty minutes a day. After a month you'll be able to concentrate a little. After six months you'll be able to block the sound out and focus like a pro. After a year, you'll be able to think quickly and accurately under any conditions—any distraction, pressure, or deadline. Soon, nothing will bother you— you'll crave more distractions. Like a New Yorker, you'll be reading the paper, talking on the phone, listening to the radio, and watching the news—all at the same time!

The same idea applies to sports. Ask a friend to blast a radio at its highest level and stand in your face screaming, while you attempt to play golf or tennis or shoot a basketball. Soon, nothing will bother you. While your opponents are distracted by a plane overhead or a child crying, you'll be playing at the top of your game! Nothing—not a rainstorm, a clap of thunder, an upset stomach, a partisan crowd—will stop you from focusing.

Finally, force yourself to think creatively under pressure by picking a day or two per month to get in your car and get lost! That's right—I said get lost on purpose! Drive to unfamiliar places without a map and try to find your way back home, without asking for help. Yes, you'll be frustrated, nervous, out of your element, aggravated. But when you arrive safely back home, you'll develop confidence in your ability to solve any problem, overcome any obstacle, and surmount any challenge. Like a New Yorker, you'll see challenges as a natural part of life.

My final New York attitude trait is to always stand up for what you believe in. Being argumentative is not a good trait—picking fights for no reason is a negative trait. But letting people know what you believe in or stand for is a positive trait. You are important. You are valuable. Your opinions count. Let the world know that you exist and your opinions matter. You are not a doormat. You will no longer sit quietly, while others lead the way. You are now a leader!

Congratulations, you are now a New York attitude addict!

Step 5: Do It with Others!

POWER PRINCIPLES

The JFK Principle

I've already told you how important it is to feel good about yourself. The JFK Principle is the other side of this coin. It involves making others feel good about themselves! It's something that confident people—like John F. Kennedy—do quite naturally. You can too. Successful individuals understand that to be successful, you'll need help. You can't do it alone. If you make others feel good—feel special—you'll create friends and fans every step of the way.

John F. Kennedy was perhaps the best all-time practitioner of this art. Polls show that JFK is ranked by the American public as one of the greatest presidents ever. The reality is that he accomplished very little in his three short years in office. He made crucial blunders—including the Bay of Pigs disaster. He was involved in numerous love affairs that almost destroyed his marriage. And he couldn't pass any major legislation—he was on lousy terms with Congress.

So why is JFK remembered so fondly? Because he made people feel good. He made us feel proud to be Americans. He exuded so much confidence, he made us feel confident about our country and ourselves. And so Americans look back on the Kennedy years as "Camelot." We remember the early sixties as the "good old days." We believed all was well in the world and our lives. Kennedy's assassination changed all that forever.

But for a few short years we were happy, proud, and confident. We stood tall.

There's a valuable lesson to be learned from John F. Kennedy. People want to feel good about themselves. People want to feel the high of confidence and pride. People want to feel special—even invincible. If you can make people feel that way, you can get people to buy anything you're selling. If you can make people feel that way, you can ask people to help you, to work for you, to follow you to the ends of the earth. If you can make people feel that way, you too will be remembered in a positive way, long after your death. If you can make people feel that way, you will be a huge success at anything you choose in life! But to make other people feel good, you have to first feel good about yourself.

The People Principle

Why is it so important to make people feel good about themselves? Because you will need their help to get ahead. You'll need people—the right people—on your side. The key to this principle is meeting the right people, at the right place, at the right time! I can't think of a more important saying for your success than, "It's not what you know, but who you know!" Connections are that important to your future success! Now I know that some people see connections as a bad word. They are the people who see the world through rose-colored glasses. They'd like the world to be a place where all that matters is talent and good ideas. They'd like to believe that people get ahead because of what they know—not who they know. But that's not the way the world really works. Connections are so important that they dwarf talent. Nothing is so common on this earth as talented people with great ideas who go nowhere with those ideas. The winner—the THRIVER—is usually the individual who has the contacts to make the great idea work!

Connections isn't a dirty word. You've had connections your whole life, literally since the moment of your birth. At that first moment, you met your doctor, a few nurses, your mother and father, then perhaps your grandparents. Before long, you were being introduced to aunts, uncles, neighbors, friends of your parents. Soon you had friends of your own to play with. You've been networking ever since—with teachers, classmates, members of the opposite sex, employees, bosses, and clients! Connections are a natural part of your fiber. We've all networked since the beginnings of time. I quote from the book *Stone Age Present* by William F. Allman:"From the beginning of time those who became leaders were not necessarily the strongest or fiercest...but those with the most friends or connections!"

> **"The opposite of networking is not working!"**
>
> *Wayne Allyn Root*

See, you can't escape this integral principle. Connections have been valuable since the beginning of time. Without friends, mentors, and role models, you can't get where you want to go! The most powerful people in the world have utilized connections to get where they wanted to go—literally from the first days on this earth. You too will need help, guidance, and tutelage every step of the way. You already understand the importance of goals. Goals are a road map to where you want to go. Think of connections as a living, breathing human version of a road map! You need to watch and learn from others to get where you want to go—just like a map!

The Charity Principle

Speaking of feeling good about yourself and treating others with respect—that brings us to the Charity Principle. Charity isn't just good for your health and the well-being of those less fortunate. It's good for business! Charity is a principle which has dramatically changed my life. The more I give of myself and my resources to others, the better I seem to do. I never look a gift horse in the mouth—I don't really care why I do so well when I enrich the lives of others. Maybe it's just a law of nature: Give to others and your success will multiply. Maybe it's God's way of rewarding generosity. Or maybe you just feel good when you give and that creates a positive attitude—which creates opportunity. I really don't know why it works. I'm just glad it does work!

If your only reservation is that you feel you can't afford to donate to charity, fear not. Whenever I could least afford to donate, that's when I gave the most. My sacrifice was always rewarded tenfold! Stretch a little. Give more than you feel you can afford. Charity is like a boomerang—it always comes back stronger than ever before.

If you really feel you don't have anything to give, donate your time at a local children's hospital. Get on the phones to raise money for your favorite charity or run a few miles in a charity race or walk-a-thon. And don't forget to recycle. It costs you nothing, yet you have the satisfaction of knowing you're leaving a better world for your children.

If you still aren't convinced that charity is your best option—because wealth and power is what your life is about—let me ask you a few questions: Why do the biggest companies in the world give so much to charity? Do you think they give away money for no reason? Do you believe celebrities donate their valuable time and talents to charitable causes simply because they want to do good?

Think again! Charity is big business and good for business. Charity is all about doing good for others, while you're doing good for yourself. Charity raises public awareness and promotes both you and your products. While advertising promotes your name too, charity does it in a subtle and more positive way. Charity enhances your image in the community. People will remember you in a warm and fuzzy way. Charity events and fund-raisers are like big networking parties. You get to meet and greet new customers, clients, and strategic partners. A good time is had by all—and they all remember your efforts on behalf of a good cause. Finally, charity brings you and your team of employees together as a family.

> **"Give and it will be given to you."**
>
> *Luke 6:38*

Positive team effort builds chemistry and loyalty. Good charitable causes and events make salespeople, employees, and executives alike proud to be a part of such a caring and community-oriented organization.

For those of you who are offended by my attempt to tie together charity and profit, I say wake up and join the real world! Charity has been used as a marketing vehicle for decades. Artists who sing at charity events for free sell millions of records due to that free exposure. Actors and entertainers who perform at telethons for free get millions of dollars in national exposure and free advertising for their careers and the television shows they star on. Yet they are also raising tens of millions of dollars for a good cause. That's what I call a win-win situation. If the result of my Charity Principle is that millions of businesspeople raise billions of dollars for good causes and their "real world" motive is to promote their companies and products—I am a very happy camper! I'm proud to have contributed to a better world.

I'm proud to have enriched the lives of those less fortunate—no matter what the ulterior motive of the donator is! Even more importantly, many of you who get involved in charity for the first time, may find that you like it. You may find it makes you feel good inside. You may get more and more involved just for the sake of doing good and enriching the lives of others! You may find that changing the lives of others changes your life for the better! No matter how you look at it, charity makes good sense—common sense and dollars and cents!

The Chicken Soup Principle

You not only need to make others feel good about themselves to succeed, you also need to make them feel guilty! I grew up with a Jewish mother, in a predominantly Italian New York neighborhood. I studied Jewish and Italian mothers up close and personal my whole childhood. These strong-willed mothers do not cook chicken soup when their children are sick because they want us to get well. They feed us, take care of us, and nurse us back to health because when we get better we will owe them—big time! It's all about guilt! You haven't truly experienced guilt until you've lived with either a Jewish or Italian mother from New York! They own the trademark for guilt!

If your goal is financial success, your job is to borrow a page from my mother's book—you must learn to cultivate guilt in the business world. Guilt works! You've got to make all the people you do business with feel guilty! Make it your job to find out the birthdays, anniversaries, and other special dates in the lives of your customers, clients, employees, and other business associates. Find out what hobbies they enjoy, what they like to do. Then reward them with flowers, cards, gifts, a bottle of fine wine, a day at an exclusive spa, tickets to a ball game, the opera, or ballet. Take them to lunch or take them golfing. What you're doing serves four distinct purposes: First, you're rewarding them for being a great boss, employee, partner, or customer. Second, you're making them feel good. Third, you're reminding them you exist. Fourth, you're making them feel guilty! Would you steal from a boss who took you and your wife out to an elegant restaurant to celebrate your anniversary? Would you switch advertising agencies, if your current account executive got you the best seats in the house for the Lakers playoff games? Would you order from a new supplier, if the old one played golf with you each Saturday?

Believe me, guilt works. It is an important part of success. When I get thoughtful gifts from clients or business associates, I am beholden. I just don't have the heart to fire a friend. I can't end a business relationship with a golfing buddy. In the real world, this is how business works. This is how business relationships are cemented. Like my Charity Principle, who cares why people do nice things for others? Who cares what the ulterior motive is? The end result is that I have built my life around the idea of doing nice things for others. If that makes others feel good and in return they reward me with business, isn't that good for everyone involved? Guilt sells! My mother was right—in chicken soup there is power!

The Conscious Capitalist Principle

Finally, my last Power Principle. This one ties together everything you must know to be a successful businessperson and a successful human being. Being a Conscious Capitalist means making money and achieving success for yourself, while doing good for others! It's simply the Golden Rule: Do unto others as you'd have others do unto you! It's an umbrella of positive principles: honesty, integrity, dignity, charity, compassion, sensitivity, and respect. It's feeling good for the success of others, instead of being jealous or bitter. It's succeeding by helping others succeed. You have a choice in life. You can choose to make money in a positive way by treating employees, clients, and customers with respect, dignity, and integrity and providing them with products that improve the world we live in. Or you can spread anger, bitterness, envy, and intimidation to the people who work for you and buy from you.

> **"The sixties was the decade of doing good. The eighties was the decade of making money. The nineties is the decade of doing good, while making money."**
>
> *Wayne Allyn Root*

My experience has been that positive is a better way to go. People that rule through manipulation and intimidation sometimes acquire great wealth, but never obtain satisfaction or peace of mind. I can think of many success icons of the decade of the eighties, who one by one have fallen by the wayside: Ivan Boeskey, Michael Milken, Leona Helmsley, Charles Keating, Mike Tyson, O. J. Simpson, Robert Maxwell, Hollywood mogul Don Simpson, even F. Lee Bailey! Did any of them seem happy? These men and women are road maps to oblivion and unhappiness.

On the other hand, there are many more examples of Conscious Capitalists who have achieved true success—who have earned huge fortunes while doing good for the world they live in. Here are just a few prominent examples:

- Anita Roddick, founder of The Body Shop

- Ben Cohen and Jerry Greenfield, founder of Ben & Jerry's Ice Cream

- Isaac Tigrett, founder of The Hard Rock Cafe and The House of Blues

- John Robbins, heir to the Baskin-Robbins Ice Cream dynasty

- Mo Siegel, founder and chairman of Celestial Seasonings

- Ardath Rodale, chairman of Rodale Press and publisher of *Prevention* magazine

- Rich DeVos and Jay Van Andel, founders of Amway Corporation

- Gerald Greenwald, CEO of United Airlines

- Leigh Steinberg, the premier agent in the world of sports

- Wayne Calloway, former CEO of Pepsico Corporation

- Bruce Kirk, Senior Vice President of Florida Crystals®

- Susi Tompkins, founder of Esprit Clothing

- Warren Buffett, CEO of Berkshire Hathaway

- Mary Kay Ash, CEO of Mary Kay Cosmetics

- Tom Chappell, CEO of Tom's of Maine

The list goes on and on. These are all multimillion-aires and business icons who choose to put people first! They empower, enlighten, and enrich the lives of the people they work with and the people who buy their products. They put the interests of their clients and customers ahead of their self-interests. They prove that when you enlighten and empower others, you really empower yourself! They prove the ultimate Power Principle—when you stress God, family, and being a human being, the money will automatically follow.

In business, choose to place your focus on creating goodwill, promoting community, encouraging the best out of employees and customers alike. Treat everyone you meet like family. Look out for the best interests of human beings—not the bottom line. I promise you the return will be a hundredfold in health, happiness, enthusiasm, confidence, self-esteem, and profits—for you and everyone and everything you touch!

POSITIVE ADDICTIONS

Be A Charity Addict

My advice on this addiction is simple: Give till it hurts! Giving to others and doing for others is really quite self-ish. That's right, I said selfish! Because every time you sacrifice for others, enlighten others, or empower others, you really empower yourself! Charity is a positive atti-tude manufacturer—you give to others and you instant-ly feel good about yourself! A positive attitude attracts success, opportunity, friends, clients, lovers—in short, everyone and everything you desire. So give, give, and give some more—and watch your self-esteem and confidence grow and glow. But be careful—smiling and laughing out loud in the middle of the day is contagious!

Here are a few ideas on making charity a scheduled part of your busy life:

- Give often—even more so when you don't feel you can afford it. I call this abundance thinking. Start to believe that you can afford to give a little more and you'll start to receive a lot more. Giving creates getting. I've found in my life that when I share with others, it comes back tenfold!

- Institute a regularly scheduled commitment to charity—either financial or physical. If you absolutely, positively can't afford it, then donate your time. Wash cars for the church or volunteer at your local Big Brothers/Big Sisters, a camp for kids with cancer, a local retirement home, hospital, or Little League.

- Donate your old furniture, cars, and clothes. You'll be helping someone less fortunate and, as a bonus, getting a healthy tax write-off too!

- Organize charity events—sports, music, celebrity—to raise money for your favorite cause. You'll be making this world a better place and exposing your company and product(s) to potential customers.

- Make someone's day today. Go out of your way to smile and say hello to strangers. Do something for one person each day without expecting anything in return!

- Recycle—the ultimate gift to our children. I'm the typical, impatient, want-it-yesterday Type A personality. I'm passionate and aggressive about everything! Once I was introduced to recycling, I became as passionate, tenacious, and committed to it as to my family and career. I love recycling. If anything, I go overboard. I'm now the recycling police! Nothing—and I mean nothing—that is recyclable gets wasted in my home or office. Recycling is like a religion to me. Every bottle, glass, or piece of paper I throw out is a chance to make this a healthier, safer, cleaner planet for my precious daughter Dakota. If you think of it in those terms, we should all be passionate about charity. Every chance you get to improve and enrich the lives of others is a chance to make this a better world for the people you love!

Be a People Addict!

You need connections to get ahead—we all do! So what's the problem? You don't know how? Are you shy? Not enough time? Are you scared to death of meeting new people? Let's answer your questions and overcome your obstacles. As far as time—like prayer, meditation, healthy diet, and all the other positive addictions—you'll have to set aside the time. Connections are so integral to your future success, you have no choice but to schedule them into your life! Schedule a set time once or twice a week to work on connections—meeting new people who can further your career or interests. If it's on your schedule, you'll do it—so schedule it! By the way, the obvious answer to a time crunch is to shut off your television twice a week. Give up the boob tube and instead become a people person. Remember, it's not what you know, it's who you know. The fact that you've watched Oprah or Ricki or Erica Kane or Jerry Seinfeld is of no use to you. Meeting people through the boob tube will not further your career. You've got to meet real live human beings—in person! So start meeting, greeting, and networking.

If your problem is that you're shy, it's time to meet your fears head-on. The only way to overcome your fears is to face them. Many of our greatest American presidents hated speaking to large crowds—yet that's precisely what they had to do to succeed. Experience the joy of failure—turn your worst fear into a positive. Force yourself to become a people person. Go out of your way to approach total strangers. Talk to everyone who'll listen to you! Cold-call potential clients and customers. Ask yourself, "What is the worst that could happen if I talk to that person?" Answer: "They ignore me and walk away." Now ask yourself, "What happens if I don't approach them at all?" Answer: "They automatically walk away." Same result. So you have absolutely nothing to lose and everything to gain from approaching anyone and everyone! If you approach twenty new people today and nineteen reject or ignore you, you've made one new friend. That's a good day! Put together a month of days like that and you'll have thirty new friends or clients! Do that for a year, you'll have 360 new friends and customers—you'll be the most popular person in town! That's the power of risk!

Finally, let me answer the "how" question—how do I make connections? The answer is a long one. Your choice is unlimited:

- Join a local, state, and/or national business organization (i.e., Chamber of Commerce, Rotary, Kiwanis, Lions Club, Young Achievers, college alumni club, Success Clubs).

- Join the local PTA (Parent-Teacher Association).

- Join a church or synagogue.

- Join a country club, tennis club, or golf club.

- Simply play golf—whether you play at public or private courses, you'll meet dozens of fellow golfers who share a wonderful passion and who might make great friends, clients, or customers.

- Join a political party and volunteer to work on local or statewide campaigns. The people you meet are all potential clients.

- Join a charity and raise funds for a good cause—the fellow fund-raisers you meet and the contributors you solicit are all potential clients, customers, employers, etc.

- Join a gym—many of the people you meet will share a common goal: improving their body, mind, and spirit!

- Offer a free column on your topic of expertise to a local newspaper or magazine. Your advice in a media setting will create credibility and attract new clients.

- Find a mentor in your field of endeavor—you might as well learn from the best. Work for free if you have to, but emulate and dissect everything he or she does. They are proven professionals at what you want to do. Remember when I worked for free for NBC Radio in New York and Chicago? Remember when I worked for the New York *Daily News* for fifty dollars per week? Those priceless lessons led to the life I lead today.

Do whatever you have to do—even for no pay—to get where you want to be or to get around the people you need to study. But by all means, do something. Take action! And stop complaining! If it is to be, it is up to me! Good luck and happy hunting.

The End

6

> **"It is never too late to be what you might have become."**
>
> *George Elliot*

Things aren't always what they appear to be. I began this book by redefining failure. I explained how failure isn't an end; often it is nothing more than a beginning—a starting point on the road to extraordinary success! I now end my book by redefining the end. I'm always sad when I finish a book. It often feels like I've lost a good friend. It's as if my subconscious is asking, "Who will keep me company now that my friend is gone?" Endings are all too often depressing, sad, and lonely. But not this one! Here the end isn't what it appears to be. In this case, the end is also a beginning. As you finish reading my book, you now have the tools to start on that magical road to extraordinary success.

As you travel that road (after reading this book, you no longer have a choice—you must travel that road) keep in mind the wise words of a legendary Italian explorer who said: "Tranquillity arrives only where the road ends." What I believe he meant was that the passion, beauty, and ecstasy of life come only when you get off the path traveled by everyone else, when you stop listening to others, when you start listening to your own inner voice. Where the road ends, it's often dusty, dirty, bumpy, even dangerous. You may bend a rim or puncture a tire. You may get stuck at the side of the road for a while. But you'll also experience highs you've never felt before. You'll learn things about life and about yourself that you never knew before. You will move forward. Only with risk comes reward, progress, and growth. Only with pain comes gain. So, in fact, tranquillity comes directly from chaos and challenge. Your goal must be to embrace failure—not run from it. You must learn how to succeed by first learning how to fail.

I have high hopes for all of you. I hope you will stay positive and motivated, committed and confident, tenacious and passionate. I hope you've learned to never give up, to never accept defeat, to never accept obstacles as immovable or odds as insurmountable, to never accept the limits of the word *no*, to never settle for a life of mediocrity. To risk and keep risking until you hear that one yes that will change your life! From this day forward, your life has changed forever—you are now a THRIVER! There is no turning back.

As I say good-bye to all of you, I want to thank you. You have given me a wonderful gift. Because of all of you who read this book, the dreams of my father—David Root—are alive once again. He's no longer afraid of failure. Every time one of you risks, every time one of you learns from a failure, every time one of you aims high, every time one of you makes the impossible possible—my father succeeds. You have enabled him to become a THRIVER! Because I've been able to pass my father's lessons on to you, he's touched the lives of thousands of readers he'll never meet. My father is now a success because of you! Long after his death, David Root will no longer be remembered as a butcher—but rather as a motivator! I can see him smiling now.

Many thanks to each of you for helping make my father's dream come true. Good luck to all of you. God bless. May all of your failures lead to extraordinary success. I'll see you at the top of the mountain at sunrise—in the black convertible Jag of course!

> I can't walk on water or part the Red Sea. I am only human. But I can choose to make the impossible possible. I can break through any wall. I will swim any ocean, climb any mountain, cross any desert, surmount any barrier, relish any challenge, conquer any obstacles standing in my way. My will, my tenacity, my determination, my drive, my commitment, and my intensity can turn my dreams into reality. And in the world we live in, that may be the greatest miracle of all!
>
> —Wayne Allyn Root

A Few Parting Words

I hope you enjoyed all my stories of miserable failure and rejection turned into extraordinary success. I'm sure you recognized many of the superachievers I call "successful failures." I'll bet you know a successful failure or two yourself—it may even be you or someone you love.

I'd love to hear from you. Please write me with your comments or your stories of lemons turned to lemonade and your "successful failure" nominees for my next book on the joy of failure! Please be sure to include your name, return address, business or home phone and fax.

Best Wishes,

Wayne Allyn Root

ROOT INTERNATIONAL
23852 Pacific Coast Hwy., Suite 372
Malibu, CA 90265
310-589-9090
888-444-ROOT (7668)
Fax: 310-589-9898
e-mail: ROOTINTL@ aol.com
or visit Wayne's worldwide web site at
http://www.wayneroot.com

Where to Get More Information

If you would like more information about Wayne Allyn Root's videotapes, audio tapes, corporate and personal seminars, keynote speeches, or private success counseling, please fill out the form on the following page and mail to:

ROOT INTERNATIONAL
23852 Pacific Coast Hwy., Suite 372
Malibu, CA 90265

310-589-9090
888-444-ROOT
Fax: 310-589-9898
e-mail: ROOTINTL@ aol.com or visit Wayne's worldwide web site at http://www.wayneroot.com

PLEASE SEND ME MORE INFORMATION ON WAYNE ALLYN ROOT'S:

__ Books

__ *Joy of Failure!* Videotapes

__ *Joy of Failure!* Audioseries

__ *Power Principles* Audioseries

__ *Success 101* Audioseries for Teenagers and Young Adults

__ *Positive Addictions* Workbook

__ Corporate seminars & keynote addresses

__ Corporate executive workshops

__ Corporate Consultation

__ Private success counseling & coaching (personalized programs created for individuals)

__ Bulk sales orders for corporations or large organizations

Name_____Company_____

Address_____

_____

Phone_____Fax_____